DUE DATE

D1510313

What's Your HI-FI Q?

From Prince to Puff Daddy, 30 Years of Black Music Trivia

SCOTT POULSON-BRYANT
AND SMOKEY D. FONTAINE

A Fireside Book

Published by Simon & Schuster

New York   London   Toronto   Sydney   Singapore

FIRESIDE
Rockefeller Center
1230 Avenue of the Americas
New York, NY 10020

FIRESIDE and colophon are registered trademarks
of Simon & Schuster Inc.

For information regarding special discounts for bulk purchases,
please contact Simon & Schuster Special Sales
at 1-800-456-6798 or business@simonandschuster.com

Designed by Michael Grant Design

All photographs courtesy of Ernie Paniccioli © 2002

Manufactured in the United States of America

10 9 8 7 6 5 4 3 2 1

Library of Congress Cataloging-in-Publication Data

Poulson-Bryant, Scott.
   What's your hi-fi Q? : from Prince to Puff Daddy, 30 years of Black music trivia / Scott Poulson-Bryant
and Smokey D. Fontaine.
      p. cm.
   1. African Americans—Music—Miscellanea.   2. Popular music—United States—Miscellanea.
I. Title: What's your hi-fi Q?.   II. Fontaine, Smokey D.   III. Title.

ML3479 .P68 2002
781.64'089'96073—dc21   2002021179
ISBN 0-7432-2955-X

ACKNOWLEDGMENTS

Many thanks to Cherise Grant at Simon & Schuster for helping to make this project so much fun. Shout-outs to La'Verne Perry-Kennedy, Chrissy Murray, Sharon Washington, Chris Chambers, Lisa Markowitz, Malika Thompson, and Karen Taylor for their welcome help. Respect to Ernie Paniccioli for keeping his lens straight all these years. Many thanks to my agent Nicole Aragi for being her fabulous self and to Nick Mullendore for being patient. Much love to Al Harmon for looking out and standing by. And to Big Smoke: Thanks for showing up at that magazine and revitalizing my music energy when my battery was starting to run low . . . and for being a good friend. As the man sang: "Style is the face U make on a Michael Jordan dunk/U got it! Style . . ."—S.P-B.

Thanks and respect are due to my mother and father for giving me the love of rhythm and blues, Cherise Grant at Simon & Schuster for having faith in a great project, Nick Mullendore and my agent Loretta Barrett, Ernie Paniccioli for spending a lifetime taking pictures, my partner in all-things music Sean Sharp, my wife Stephanie for her tireless support of a late-night writer, and Scott Poulson-Bryant for being the best mentor an intern could have ever asked for.—S.D.F.

THE INTRO

Do you know your HI-FI Q?

We gather that since you picked up this book, you must like music. More than that, you must like the minutiae of music—the who, what, why, how, and when of music. You're probably interested in who writes the songs and who produces them, who sings the background vocals and who arranges them. You're probably as into the rhythm of the backbeat as you are the rhythms of the recording sessions.

Or maybe not. Maybe you just like trivia; you just like to be the smartest person in the room. You thought, like we did, that the world of trivia needed some funk, some color, some real, honest-to-goodness GAME. That's fine. This book is for folks like you, too.

This book actually started years ago, when the two of us were at *VIBE* magazine, stuck in a tiny office together, trying to get through the day. We'd ask each other questions about music:

"Did you know that Prince's *Lovesexy* CD was programmed as one long track?"

"No doubt. Do you know what song Puffy sampled for Mary's record?"

And on and on. That's what happens when you're straight-up musicheads, when the CD in your portable player defines the day you're having, when the gifts you give to members of your wedding party are definitive Prince mix-CDs, when almost every article you write opens with a quote from some song you can't get out of your head.

No trivia book is complete without some lists, so we've included a few. Running throughout, we've offered up Scott and Smokey's Totally Biased and Subjective Choices for the Best Albums and Singles over the last three decades. We welcome your disagreements. Also, check out the celebrity lists. We asked some celebs what they consider to be the best records over the last few years. See what they think.

So, we ask again: Do you know your HI-FI Q? Do you know how much trivia you're carrying around in that music-addled brain of yours, slurped up from years of watching MTV or reading music magazines or listening to interviews with your favorite artists? Maybe you do, maybe you don't. But if you're still reading this far, you probably do want to know your HI-FI Q . . . and you probably want to test yours against all the other musicheads in your midst.

We've divided the book up into three sections—the discofied seventies, the crossover eighties, the hip-hoppin' nineties—so that we'd give you some breadth against which to test your mettle. You can't call yourself a true musichead if all you know about are the couple of artists who rocked your world around the time you were losing your virginity. Nah, you gotta have a variety of knowledge that astounds your friends and annoys your enemies; you gotta be able to speak all the music slanguages that define who we are.

In each section, the questions start out pretty easy and become more difficult. Pointwise, they go from 1 point to 2 points to 5 points, 5-pointers being the hardest questions of the bunch. If you answer all the questions right, you score an amazing 1,000 points and earn a definitive position as the Highest HI-FI Qer in your 'hood. There are even some bonus questions, but you have to go to the HI-FI Q Web site (www.hifiq.com or www.blackbookscentral.com) to get to those answers. But that's for later. Let's not get ahead of ourselves.

So, go. Get a pen or a pencil, or a crayon for all we care. Sharpen it up as you sharpen up your brain to dive into the test at hand.

At the end, you'll know your HI-FI Q. And you'll be glad that you do.

Are you ready? All right, as the song says: "Put the needle on the record."

What's Your HI-FI Q?

Press Play

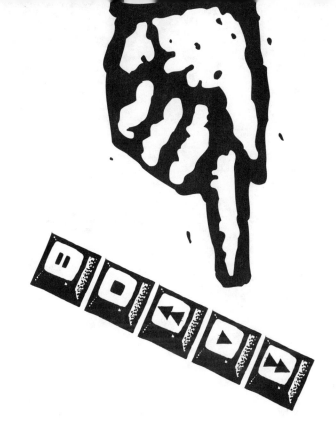

QUINCY JONES

THE 70s

Disco, Decadence, and Designer Jeans

What's Your HI-FI Q?

THE SEVENTIES: DISCO, DECADENCE, AND DESIGNER JEANS

The seventies . . . the decade that celebrated designer jeans and denim suits, disco balls and skating halls, leisure suits and chukka boots, and Alex Haley's *Roots*. Pop culture exploded like something in a *Star Wars* movie, and even though the government seemed to be imploding, black music was thriving like it hadn't since the birth of the blues.

This was the decade of disco, of die-hard decadence, of the polyestered pursuit of happiness on the dance floor. *Saturday Night Fever* took it mainstream, but loving the nightlife, the "burn-baby-burn" energy of it, became a cultural conceit of its own, encouraging 12-inch remixes of dance hits that gave epic scope to songs that only wanted to make us feel good. This was the decade when Donna Summer orgasmically moaned her way through 17 minutes of a Euro-trance beat—and had a hit record in the process.

Berry Gordy's Motown was entering another decade of dominance, as recording artists committed their innervisions to wax, asking the world "what's going on?" instead of being "too busy thinking about my baby." Stevie Wonder and Marvin Gaye, pop stars both, were among the artists who found their true voices in the seventies, metamorphosing into artists who were looking at the world around them and finding righteousness in the rhythms of the everyday. Even the mighty Temptations had grown, from "My Girl" to the politics and gritty realism of "Ball of Confusion (That's What the World Is Today)" and "Papa Was a Rollin' Stone."

And rumbling underneath all of this, on the corners and around the blocks, there were the breakbeat concertos of rap music scratching their way to the surface. Chic's "Good Times" was becoming the backbeat to a movement that understood the irony of downtown folks spending crazy dollars to get into a club when the red-lighted basement party of the folks next door would do just fine. Two turntables and a microphone could get a party started, and more often than not, did.

What do you think about when you think about the seventies?

Answer some of these questions and see if your memories are as strong as a Bernard Edwards bass line.

What's Your HI-FI Q?

SCOTT'S #**10** PICK FOR BEST SINGLES OF THE 1970s:

"What's Going On,"
Marvin Gaye (1971)

Touching, topical, sublimely sung—one of the best background sounds to hit vinyl. A party to save the world.

SCOTT'S #**9** PICK FOR BEST SINGLES OF THE 1970s:

"I'll Be There," Jackson 5 (1970)

I'll put it to you this way: Mariah Carey's cover was absolutely unnecessary. Michael Jackson's high notes define male yearning. This is where you really knew what MJ had in him.

GENERAL INTEREST

Here are some questions to get you going; to warm you up, as it were. So go ahead, crack those knuckles, set your brain on that groovy ol' seventies vibe and get ready to find out how high your HI-FI Q is. Remember, the questions will get harder as you go deeper into the groove. So get set . . . go! Or as Aretha Franklin might put it: "Jump to It."

1. Which artist spent five years as Dorothy in the Broadway stage production of *The Wiz?*
   a) Diana Ross
   b) Stephanie Mills
   c) Irene Cara
   d) Janet Jackson

2. In 1970, Teddy Pendergrass replaced the lead singer of which group?
   a) the Temptations
   b) the Commodores
   c) Harold Melvin and the Blue Notes
   d) Earth, Wind & Fire

3. According to Gladys Knight and the Pips, "Neither One of Us" wants to be the first to do what?
   a) clean the house
   b) say good-bye
   c) go to the cleaners
   d) call it a day

4. What kind of animal was Michael Jackson singing to in "Ben"?
   a) a rabbit
   b) a pony
   c) a rat
   d) a frog

5. Michael Jackson's seventies hit "Got to Be There" was remade in 1982 by what soul diva?

a) Patti LaBelle
b) Chaka Khan
c) Evelyn "Champagne" King
d) Gladys Knight

6. The initials in the disco hit "TSOP" stand for "The Sound Of" what?

a) Puerto Rico
b) Philadelphia
c) Portland
d) Privacy

7. Steveland Morris is better known as whom?

a) Steve Arrington
b) Stevie Wonder
c) Smokey Robinson
d) Ike Turner

8. Which of the following groups was NOT a family act?

a) the Sylvers
b) DeBarge
c) Rose Royce
d) Sister Sledge

9. Which Roberta Flack single was a remake of a Shirelles' hit?

a) "Killing Me Softly With His Song"
b) "Will You Love Me Tomorrow"
c) "Jesse"
d) "Where Is the Love"

[Answers on page 52]

SMOKEY'S #10 PICK FOR BEST SINGLES OF THE 1970s:

"Apache," The Incredible Bongo Band (1973)

This cornucopia of psychedelic keyboards, conga drums, and spaghetti western–like trumpet playing became one of the main building blocks of the break-dancing movement. Thirty years later, every riff in this manic workout will still incite spontaneous acts of back-spinning at a park near you.

SMOKEY'S #9 PICK FOR BEST SINGLES OF THE 1970s:

"Got to Be Real," Cheryl Lynn (1979)

One of the funkiest disco records of its age, Cheryl Lynn's high-pitched scream is well matched by the high-energy trumpets that waste no time getting to the land of hoopin' and hollerin'. Love should always have this kind of brass accompaniment. Sweat the night away or simply leave the building.

DIANA ROSS

10. Diana Ross's "Ain't No Mountain High Enough" was a remake of a song by which Motown duo?

    a) Marvin Gaye and Tammi Terrell
    b) Marvin Gaye and Kim Weston
    c) Michael Jackson and Mary Wells
    d) Smokey Robinson and Tammi Terrell

11. Who had a disco hit with a new version of the Jackson 5's "Never Can Say Goodbye"?

    a) Donna Summer
    b) Gloria Gaynor
    c) Maxine Nightingale
    d) Teena Marie

12. Which "Boogie" song was released first?

    a) "Boogie Nights," by Heatwave
    b) "Get Up and Boogie (That's Right)," by Silver Convention
    c) "Boogie Fever," by the Sylvers
    d) "Boogie Down," by Eddie Kendricks

13. Which of these "Star" songs came out first?

    a) "Star Love," by Cheryl Lynn
    b) "Wishin' On a Star," by Rose Royce
    c) "You Don't Have to Be a Star (To Be in My Show)," by Marilyn McCoo and Billy Davis, Jr.
    d) "Baby, I'm a Star," by Prince

14. Which of these "Love" songs came out first?

    a) "Love to Love You Baby," by Donna Summer
    b) "Love All the Hurt Away," by Aretha Franklin
    c) "Love Hangover," by Diana Ross
    d) "Love Train," by the O'Jays

[Answers on page 52]

SCOTT'S #10 PICK FOR
BEST ALBUMS OF THE 1970s:

Saturday Night Fever soundtrack, *various artists (1977)*

Because it personified mainstream disco in a way that didn't look down its nose at the originators. Because it was funky enough to be the soundtrack to any party you wanted to go to. Because Yvonne Elliman was fly. Because "You Should Be Dancing" rumbles by on a beat that sounds heaven sent. Because it felt like New York on vinyl. Because the movie turned me out. Because "How Deep Is Your Love" is one of the all-time best seventies ballads. Because it gave John Travolta a beat he could groove to. And it made white boys hip.

9

What's Your HI-FI Q?

15. On what 1976 Stevie Wonder album will you find the sample Coolio used on "Gangsta's Paradise"?
    a) Music of My Mind
    b) Innervisions
    c) Songs in the Key of Life
    d) In Square Circle

16. Which of these "Do" songs came out first?
    a) "Do You Love What You Feel," by Rufus featuring Chaka Khan
    b) "Do Right Woman, Do Right Man," by Aretha Franklin
    c) "Do I Do," by Stevie Wonder
    d) "Do It ('Til You're Satisfied)," by B.T. Express

17. Yvette Marie Stevens is better known as whom?
    a) Natalie Cole
    b) Chaka Khan
    c) Marilyn McCoo
    d) Tina Turner

18. Which Aretha Franklin hit was NOT a remake?
    a) "Spanish Harlem"
    b) "Respect"
    c) "Don't Play That Song"
    d) "Border Song"

19. Which "Number" song was released first?
    a) "One Less Bell to Answer," by the Fifth Dimension
    b) "Just the Two of Us," by Grover Washington, Jr. (with Bill Withers)
    c) "Three Times a Lady," by the Commodores
    d) "50 Ways to Leave Your Lover," by Paul Simon

SCOTT'S #8 PICK FOR BEST SINGLES OF THE 1970s:

"Rock Steady,"
Aretha Franklin (1971)

One of Ree's finest seventies moments. Sure-footed and solid, an uptempo rhythm machine that won't cut off.

20. Which seventies Stylistics ballad has been covered by both Prince and Phyllis Hyman?

a) "You Make Me Feel Brand New"
b) "Let's Put It All Together"
c) "Betcha by Golly, Wow"
d) "You Are Everything"

21. Who recorded the original seventies hit "Mr. Big Stuff"?

a) Loleatta Holloway
b) Jean Carne
c) Jean Knight
d) Phyllis Hyman

22. What was the first Philly soul production by Gamble and Huff to go to Number One on the pop charts?

a) "Me and Mrs. Jones," by Billy Paul
b) "When Will I See You Again," by the Three Degrees
c) "Backstabbers," by the O'Jays
d) "Enjoy Yourself," by the Jacksons

23. Chic's "Le Freak" was written the night that the group was turned away from which Manhattan nightclub?

a) Palladium
b) Studio 54
c) Bentley's
d) The Copacabana

24. Which Marvin Gaye album chronicled his love affair with and divorce from Anna Gordy?

a) *Let's Get It On*
b) *Here, My Dear*
c) *What's Going On*
d) *In Our Lifetime*

[Answers on page 52]

SMOKEY'S #**8** PICK FOR
BEST SINGLES OF THE 1970s:

"Celebration,"
Kool & the Gang (1979)

With its driving bass line and fierce horn section, this was more than simply the overused anthem it is today. This was funk, Kool & the Gang funk, the likes of which few other bands have ever kept up. For better or for worse, this song will never go out of style. Isn't that the true definition of a classic?

11

NILE RODGERS

25. The Jackson 5's "The Love You Save" was originally written about what? `2 points`

a) a bank account
b) traffic safety
c) a dice game
d) a movie star

26. Stevie Wonder was awarded a Grammy for Album of the Year two years in a row for which albums?

a) *Fulfillingness' First Finale* and *Innervisions*
b) *Songs in the Key of Life* and *Hotter Than July*
c) *Hotter Than July* and *In Square Circle*
d) *Innervisions* and *In Square Circle*

BONUS INTERNET QUESTION: The next album Stevie recorded also won Best Album of the Year. Can you name it?

27. Who did Stevie Wonder present to audiences when her debut was released in 1974? `2 points`

a) Minnie Riperton
b) Syreeta
c) Natalie Cole
d) Amii Stewart

28. Which Barbra Streisand hit did Gladys Knight remake, blending it with "Try to Remember"? `2 points`

a) "Evergreen"
b) "The Way We Were"
c) "The Main Event"
d) "New York State of Mind"

SMOKEY'S # **10** PICK FOR
BEST ALBUMS OF THE 1970s:

Let's Get It On, *Marvin Gaye (1973)*

After Marvin laid this score, lovemaking was no longer possible for a brother if you didn't have this record cued and ready. One of the most satisfying bedroom albums ever put to wax, these eight songs oozed with the lust of a soul master. The horns blared passion, the string arrangements soared to climax, and Marvin's crooning would never be more convincing.

Essential tracks: "Distant Lover" and "Keep Gettin' It On."

[Answers on page 52]

GEORGE CLINTON

29. **Name two Parliament/Funkadelic spin-off groups whose members once played with George Clinton:**

a) the Revolution and New Power Generation
b) Goodie Mob and OutKast
c) Brides of Funkenstein and Bootsy's Rubber Band
d) Funkdoobiest and Cypress Hill

30. **Who recorded the anti-Vietnam War anthem "Bring the Boys Home"?** `2 points`

a) Freda Payne
b) Thelma Houston
c) Tina Turner
d) Stacy Lattisaw

31. **Which Jackson 5 single peaked at Number Two on the charts, thus ending their reign of four straight number one hits?** `2 points`

a) "Dancing Machine"
b) "Mama's Pearl"
c) "Never Can Say Goodbye"
d) "Maybe Tomorrow"

32. **In 1979, the Grammy category Best Disco Recording was awarded for the first time. Who won?** `2 points`

a) Donna Summer for "Hot Stuff"
b) Gloria Gaynor for "I Will Survive"
c) Diana Ross for "Love Hangover"
d) Sister Sledge for "We Are Family"

33. **Boyz II Men's "It's So Hard to Say Goodbye to Yesterday" was a remake of whose 1975 *Cooley High* soundtrack song?** `2 points`

a) G.C. Cameron
b) Marvin Gaye
c) Chairmen of the Board
d) the Stylistics

[Answers on page 52]

SCOTT'S **#9** PICK FOR BEST ALBUMS OF THE 1970s:

Nightbirds, *Labelle* (1974)

Produced by New Orleans master Allen Touissant, this is Labelle's finest record. Brusque and sexy, smart and occasionally silly, Nightbirds contains three of the finest Labelle performances committed to vinyl: the classic "Lady Marmalade," the viscerally defiant "What Can I Do for You," and the seethingly seductive "You Turn Me On." Patti was at her shouting, rambunctious best; Sarah Dash colored the vocal lines with her usual sinuous trills; and Nona, crazy old fabulous Nona Hendryx, swooped all over the place, anchoring the trio with a muscular authority. Spry, decadent, flamboyantly fun, and strutting like the beautiful birds they were, Labelle created music for the peacock in you.

What's Your HI-FI Q?

34. Who won the Best R&B Vocal Performance, Female Grammy every year between 1967 and 1974? `2 points`

  a) Diana Ross
  b) Aretha Franklin
  c) Gladys Knight
  d) Dionne Warwick

BONUS INTERNET QUESTION: Who broke her string of wins?

35. Earth, Wind & Fire's "Got to Get You Into My Life" was written and recorded originally by which British group? `2 points`

  a) the Rolling Stones
  b) the Who
  c) the Beatles
  d) the Kinks

36. Which of these singers has NOT remade a Beatles song? `2 points`

  a) Chaka Khan
  b) Aretha Franklin
  c) Tina Turner
  d) Cherrelle

LYRICALLY SPEAKING

Now we'll see how much you listen when you're crooning along to the oldies station (shout-out to Jammin' 105.1 in N.Y.C.!). Of course, you can sing along if you think that'll help jog your memory to answer this set of questions. Or, as Earth, Wind & Fire might put it . . . "sing a soooongggg." They get harder as you get deeper.

37. "Inner City Blues" made Marvin Gaye want to do what?

  a) holler
  b) scream
  c) yell
  d) contort

38. According to which song, where is it that "There ain't no tellin' who you might meet/A movie star or maybe even an Indian chief . . ."?

a) "Funkytown"
b) "In the Navy"
c) "Car Wash"
d) "Y.M.C.A."

39. On which movie soundtrack did Curtis Mayfield declare, "I'm your mother, I'm your daddy, I'm that nigga in the alley"?

a) *Shaft*
b) *Superfly*
c) *Shaft in Africa*
d) *Coffy*

40. Which song starts, "At first I was afraid I was petrified/Kept thinkin' I could never live without you by my side . . ."?

a) "The Boss"
b) "No One Gets the Prize"
c) "I Will Survive"
d) "Got to Be Real"

41. Which Chic song says, "Happy days are here again/The time is right for making friends . . ."?

a) "Le Freak"
b) "Good Times"
c) "I Want Your Love"
d) "Everybody Dance"

SMOKEY'S #**7** PICK FOR
BEST SINGLES OF THE 1970s:

"Best Thing That's Ever Happened to Me," Gladys Knight & the Pips (1973)

When you look back on life, what will you see? Above all, hopefully you'll have a reason to sing a song like this. "I've had my share of life's ups and downs/but fate's been kind, the downs have been few." That Gladys's joy to have been in love is balanced by some of life's more sobering realities makes this psalm all the more real. A soul singer's best work and Lena's favorite.

[Answers on page 52]

ISAAC HAYES

42. Which Oscar-winning song describes the lead character as, " ... the black private dick/That's a sex machine with all the chicks?"

a) "Macho Man"
b) "Trouble Man"
c) "Superfly"
d) "Shaft"

43. Which anthem told us, "There's been so many things that's held us down/But now it looks like things are finally comin' around"?

a) "Celebration"
c) "Turn the Beat Around"
b) "Ain't No Stoppin' Us Now"
d) "What's Going On"

44. Which song describes a woman fine enough to "Make an old man wish for younger days"?

a) "Ladies Night"
b) "Brick House"
c) "Lady Marmalade"
d) "Heaven Must Be Missing an Angel"

45. Which song tells us, "We're all sensitive people/With so much to give"?

a) "Distant Lover"
b) "Let's Get It On"
c) "Sail On"
d) "Me and Mrs. Jones"

46. Which song starts, "Music is a world within itself/With a language we all understand"?

a) "I Wish"
b) "Glow of Love"
c) "Sir Duke"
d) "Love Machine"

[Answers on page 52]

SMOKEY'S #**9** PICK FOR BEST ALBUMS OF THE 1970s:

There's a Riot Goin' On, Sly and the Family Stone (1971)

Released just months after Marvin's What's Going On *LP, this was Sly's sorrow song for the ages. It was as if the members of his band, now somehow stripped of the joy their lives once held, forced themselves to reduce their earlier feel-good hits to a set of haunting, middle-Earth grooves. Why was the sadness so captivating? Years later, only hip-hop's nihilistic lyrics would provoke the same question.*

Essential tracks: "Family Affair" and "Thank You for Talkin' to me Africa."

What's Your HI-FI Q?

47. Which song begins, "Sittin' here eatin' my heart out/ Waitin' for some lover to call"?
    a) "Bad Girls"
    b) "On the Radio"
    c) "Hot Stuff"
    d) "Mr. Big Stuff"

48. Which song starts, "I will love you anyway/Even if you cannot stay"?
    a) "Stay"
    b) "Native New Yorker"
    c) "Sweet Thing"
    d) "Don't Leave Me This Way"

49. Which song tells us, "Our voices will ring together/Until the twelfth of never"?
    a) "Fantasy"
    b) "Let's Groove"
    c) "Boogie Wonderland"
    d) "Can You Feel It?"

50. Which song starts with, "L.A. proved too much for the man/So he's leavin' the life he's come to know"?
    a) "Midnight Train to Georgia"
    b) "Hot Line"
    c) "Hollywood"
    d) "Hollywood Swinging"

51. According to Cornelius Brothers and Sister Rose, "you gotta treat her like" what?
    a) a prostitute
    b) a lady
    c) a friend
    d) a liar

52. **What seventies song stated "Every day the sun comes up around her/She can make the birds sing harmony"?**

a) the O'Jays' "Usedta Be My Girl"
b) the Four Tops' "Ain't No Woman (Like the One I Got)"
c) the Commodores' "Brick House"
d) Barry White's "Never Never Gonna Give Ya Up"

53. **Who sang these lyrics in 1979: "I'm caught up in a one night love affair/Hopin' true love will find me there"?** `2 points`

a) Inner Life
b) Inner Circle
c) Inner Spirit
d) Inner Groove

54. **Who wants to be a "Superwoman" in Stevie Wonder's song of that name?** `2 points`

a) Lisa
b) Maggie
c) Mary
d) Angie

55. **Which song starts with a chant of "Burn, baby, burn!"?** `2 points`

a) "Fire and Desire"
b) "Disco Inferno"
c) "Burn This Disco Out"
d) "Boogie Fever"

56. **Which song begins, "What's the sense in sharing, this one and only life/Ending up, just another lost and lonely wife"?** `2 points`

a) "Young Love"
b) "Young Hearts Run Free"
c) "When You're Young and in Love"
d) "P.Y.T. (Pretty Young Thing)"

[Answers on page 52]

SMOKEY'S #**6** PICK FOR BEST SINGLES OF THE 1970s:

"(Not Just) Knee Deep (Pts. I & II)," Funkadelic (1979)

Perhaps the best example of George Clinton's Parliament/ Funkadelic everything-but-the-kitchen-sink sound—at least for the dance floor—this funk workout features a thick, ugly bass line, an incredibly catchy call-and-response hook, and of course some very tasty lyrics. I love the way George's Greek chorus tries to hide itself slightly behind the groove.

SMOKEY'S #**5** PICK FOR BEST SINGLES OF THE 1970s:

"I Want You Back," Jackson 5 (1970)

The opening piano notes have been sampled so often that on first listen, Michael and the gang's pubescent wailings sound trite. But think of how many jams couldn't have existed without this as its parent, or the pleas of a young gloved one you other-wise never would have heard.

SISTER SLEDGE

57. What else do we know about the boy whose body "would shame Adonis"? `2 points`

a) "He's So Shy"
b) "He's the Greatest Dancer"
c) "He's Got the Whole World in His Hands"
d) "He's Strange"

58. What seventies girl group sang these lyrics: "Experience in love preferred, but will accept a young trainee"? `2 points`

a) Love Unlimited
b) Labelle
c) the Supremes
d) Honey Cone

LIGHTS, CAMERA, *SOUNDTRACK*

In this section, all the questions are related to those great soundtracks that crammed the shelves back in the day. Remember when Curtis, Isaac, and Marvin were making records that were better than the flix they came from? If you don't, we suggest you boogie to the video store and catch up.

59. Donna Summer's "Last Dance" appeared in which film?

a) *Saturday Night Fever*
b) *Xanadu*
c) *Thank God, It's Friday*
d) *Can't Stop the Music*

60. What is the theme song to *Mahogany*?

a) "Touch Me in the Morning"
b) "Do You Know Where You're Going To"
c) "Reach Out and Touch Someone's Hand"
d) "Ain't No Mountain High Enough"

[Answers on page 52]

SCOTT'S #**8** PICK FOR BEST ALBUMS OF THE 1970s:

The Boss, *Diana Ross (1979)*

This is the album where Ashford and Simpson—two of the finest songwriters in the pop/R&B idiom—take Diana higher. Miss Ross sings her ass off through a gospel of relationship truths that make her sound like a preacher on the mount. This is sublime, middle-period Diana; Studio 54, "baby-I'm-a-star" Diana. This is the album where Diana sings like a lady with the blues, but with enough rhythm to shake those blues away and enjoy herself. Check out the ad-libs on "No One Gets the Prize"—Diana was never better. Love taught her (and she taught us) who, indeed, was the Boss.

Essential tracks: "The Boss" and "It's My House."

23

What's Your HI-FI Q?

61. Which family group recorded the title song to the film *Let's Do It Again*?

a) Sister Sledge
b) the Staple Singers
c) the Isley Brothers
d) the Jackson 5

62. Who wrote and produced Aretha Franklin's 1977 *Sparkle* soundtrack?

a) Quincy Jones
b) Curtis Mayfield
c) Isaac Hayes
d) Faith Evans

63. For which Francis Ford Coppola-directed film did Stevie Wonder cowrite and record the theme song? `2 points`

a) *The Godfather*
b) *The Outsiders*
c) *Peggy Sue Got Married*
d) *Gardens of Stone*

64. Which song did Michael Jackson sing with the crows in *The Wiz*? `2 points`

a) "You Can't Win"
b) "Leave Me Alone"
c) "Steppin' to the Bad Side"
d) "Black & White"

65. On which motion picture soundtrack did Stevie Wonder NOT perform? `2 points`

a) *Jungle Fever*
b) *Silver Streak*
c) *The Woman in Red*
d) *The Secret Life of Plants*

SCOTT'S **#4** PICK FOR BEST SINGLES OF THE 1970s:

"Native New Yorker," Odyssey (1977)

The world-weary coke high feels built right into the groove. And how can you resist sentiment like: "You're no tramp, but you're no lady, talkin' that street talk/You're the heart and soul of New York City?"

COMPARE AND CONTRAST (ANALOGIES)

What's a test without some analogies to keep you on your toes? You know, this is to that as that is to this? Here are some analogies that should keep you occupied for a little while. Or, as Black Sheep might say: "You can get with this or you can get with that."

66. Diana Ross is to *Lady Sings the Blues* as Gladys Knight is to:

a) *Mahogany*
b) *Pipe Dreams*
c) *Claudine*
d) *Sounder*

67. Gladys Knight is to the Pips as Martha Reeves is to:

a) the Miracles
b) the Supremes
c) the Vandellas
d) the Temptations

68. The Spinners are to "The Rubberband Man" as Sammy Davis, Jr., is to:

a) "The Trouble Man"
b) "The Ice-Cream Man"
c) "The Flimflam Man"
d) "The Candy Man"

69. Johnnie Taylor is to "Disco Lady" as Stevie Wonder is to:

a) "Ladies' Night"
b) "Golden Lady"
c) "Lady Marmalade"
d) "The Lady in My Life"

SMOKEY'S **#4** PICK FOR
BEST SINGLES OF THE 1970s:

"Close the Door,"
Teddy Pendergrass (1978)

This time the great Gamble and Huff use only a string section to match the vocal power of Teddy P. "I've waited all day long" the workerman purrs, his passion rising as the track rolls to an obvious climax. Next to "Let's Get It On," this was, without question, the decade's finest sexual invitation. But Teddy was rougher than Marvin; wait for the growls at the end of the conquest to appreciate the song's real nerve. "Come here, woman!"

[Answers on page 52]

CHAKA KHAN

70. George McCrae is to "Rock Your Baby" as Gwen McCrae is to:

a) "Rock the Boat"
b) "Rock With You"
c) "Rockin' Robin"
d) "Rockin' Chair"

71. Stevie Wonder is to Rufus's "Tell Me Something Good" as Rick James is to:

a) the Mary Jane Girls'"All Night Long"
b) the Weather Girls'"It's Raining Men"
c) the Pointer Sisters'"I'm So Excited"
d) the Jones' Girls'"One Night Love Affair"

72. Aretha Franklin is to "Bridge Over Troubled Water" as Jermaine Jackson is to:

a) "Parsely, Sage, Rosemary and Thyme"
b) "Mrs. Robinson"
c) "50 Ways to Leave Your Lover"
d) "The Boxer"

73. Tina Turner is to "Let's Stay Together" as Chaka Khan is to:
2 points

a) "Any Old Sunday"
b) "I Feel for You"
c) "I'm Every Woman"
d) "Clouds"

SMOKEY'S #8 PICK FOR
BEST ALBUMS OF THE 1970s:

The Best of Earth, Wind & Fire, Vol. 1, *Earth, Wind & Fire (1978)*

More like a jam-filled mixtape than your typical end-of-career retrospective, this—the second of two greatest-hits packages on this list— was a triumphant presentation of Philip Bailey's falsetto beauty and bandleader Maurice White's natural understanding of what makes a good song. Rhythm and blues has never had a better set of melodies. And just imagine, the songs actually meant something.

Essential tracks: "Shining Star," "Reasons," and "Fantasy."

What's Your HI-FI Q?

"AND NOW I'D LIKE TO INTRODUCE THE BAND . . ."

In this section, the questions are related to group, bands, and duets. Remember bands? When everyone played an instrument and knew how to put on a show? What? You don't? Then maybe you should bypass this section. Coward . . . Or as the bandleader says: "And-a one, and-a two . . ."

74. Marilyn McCoo and Billy Davis, Jr., recorded "You Don't Have to Be a Star (To Be in My Show)" after leaving which seventies pop/R&B group?
   a) the Fifth Dimension
   b) the Friends of Distinction
   c) the Miracles
   d) Cornelius Brothers and Sister Rose

75. The Hues Corporation had their biggest hit with a disco song called what?
   a) "Rock Me Baby"
   b) "Rockin' Chair"
   c) "Rock the Boat"
   d) "Rock Me Gently"

76. Jeffrey Osbourne sang lead for which group before going solo?
   a) the Bar-Kays
   b) LTD
   c) the Gap Band
   d) Maze

77. The members of the Commodores met and formed at which historically black college?
   a) Hampton Institute
   b) Tuskegee Institute
   c) Fisk University
   d) Howard University

78. **Which singer was never a member of Wonderlove, Stevie Wonder's backup group?**

   a) Minnie Riperton
   b) Deniece Williams
   c) Syreeta
   d) Freda Payne

79. **After a string of solo hits, Dionne Warwick made "Then Came You" with which group?** `2 points`

   a) the Spinners
   b) the Whispers
   c) the Jacksons
   d) the Temptations

80. **Roberta Flack and Donny Hathaway were classmates at which historically black college?** `2 points`

   a) Howard University
   b) Lincoln University
   c) Fisk University
   d) Clark College

81. **What was the name of Sylvester's background singers?** `2 points`

   a) Mighty Clouds of Joy
   b) Two Tons O' Fun
   c) Odyssey
   d) the Weather Girls

82. **With whom does Marvin Gaye duet on "My Mistake (Was to Love You)"?** `2 points`

   a) Kim Weston
   b) Diana Ross
   c) Tammi Terrell
   d) Jean Terrell

SMOKEY'S #**7** PICK FOR
BEST ALBUMS OF THE 1970s:

On the Radio: Greatest Hits, Vols. I & II, *Donna Summer (1979)*

It was billed as a greatest hits package, but the rocking new title cut proved that this dancing queen hadn't finished making her mark on the decade. Whenever the orgasmic soul of "Love to Love You Baby" can ride next to the grinding electronica of "I Feel Love," and the funk opera of "MacArthur Park" leads into burners like "Hot Stuff" and "Bad Girls," just throw up the white flag. Donna, baby, you win!

Essential tracks: "Heaven Knows" and "Dim All the Lights."

[Answers on page 53]

What's Your HI-FI Q?

SCOTT'S #6 PICK FOR BEST ALBUMS OF THE 1970s:

Sparkle soundtrack, *Aretha Franklin and Curtis Mayfield* (1976)

The movie was solid, old-fashioned Hollywood entertainment; the soundtrack redefined what soundtracks were and had to be. Curtis Mayfield supplied Aretha with the finest songs she'd sung in years and pretty much relaunched her flagging career with this wondrously vivid work of art. In Aretha's soul-sister shouts, Curtis Mayfield's hypernarrative songwriting style found a lissome voice to give life to his world-weary words. Lonette McKee and Irene Cara may have performed the jams on screen, but on wax, Aretha owned this material like she hadn't in years.

Essential tracks: "Jump" and "Giving Him Something He Could Feel."

83. Which seventies female R&B group recorded an album with pop star Laura Nyro? `2 points`
    a) the Supremes
    b) Labelle
    c) Sister Sledge
    d) the Three Degrees

84. Luther Vandross sang and arranged backing vocals for which British singer? `2 points`
    a) Cliff Richard
    b) David Bowie
    c) Tom Jones
    d) Phil Collins

85. Lou Rawls sang backing vocals for which fifties pop/R&B icon? `2 points`
    a) Nat "King" Cole
    b) Sam Cooke
    c) Frankie Lymon
    d) Jackie Wilson

86. Who sang the hook on Toto's "Georgie Porgie"? `2 points`
    a) Chaka Khan
    b) Cheryl Lynn
    c) Gwen Guthrie
    d) Jocelyn Brown

87. Rod Temperton, writer of hits "Rock With You" and "Baby Come to Me," was keyboardist for which group? `2 points`
    a) Heatwave
    b) Kool & the Gang
    c) Earth, Wind & Fire
    d) KC and the Sunshine Band

THEY WRITE THE SONGS (SONGWRITING)

88. **Which star wrote Jermaine Jackson's "Let's Get Serious"?**

   a) Stevie Wonder
   b) Michael Jackson
   c) Lionel Richie
   d) Luther Vandross

89. **Which noted songwriting team wrote Sister Sledge's "We Are Family"?**

   a) Kenny Gamble and Leon Huff
   b) Nile Rodgers and Bernard Edwards
   c) Linda Creed and Thom Bell
   d) Reggie Lucas and James Mtume

90. **Which rock star wrote the Pointer Sisters' hit cover "Fire"?**

   a) Elton John
   b) Bruce Springsteen
   c) Mick Jagger
   d) Elvis Presley

91. **Who wrote Aretha Franklin's "Until You Come Back to Me"?**

   a) Curtis Mayfield
   b) Stevie Wonder
   c) Quincy Jones
   d) Marvin Gaye

92. **Which TV star wrote the song "Never Can Say Goodbye"?**

   a) Clifton Davis
   b) Demond Wilson
   c) Nipsy Russell
   d) John Amos

SMOKEY'S #**6** PICK FOR
BEST ALBUMS OF THE 1970s:

Saturday Night Fever soundtrack, *various artists (1977)*

This double-album LP permanently changed the musical landscape when it brought disco to the dance floor in a white polyester suit. The hits from this album never stopped, with The Bee Gees' and their falsetto purring scoring no less than six Top 10 singles. But these songs weren't just for dancing—they became a guidebook for life itself.

Essential tracks: "Stayin' Alive," "Night Fever," and "Disco Inferno."

[Answers on page 53]

PHYLLIS HYMAN

93. Phyllis Hyman was a featured singer for which noted composer/producer?

a) Quincy Jones
b) Norman Connors
c) Curtis Mayfield
d) Burt Bacharach

94. Which R&B star shared credit on a Beatles song? `2 points`

a) Billy Preston
b) Stevie Wonder
c) Michael Jackson
d) Marvin Gaye

95. Which girl group played the Wilson Sisters in the movie *Car Wash*? `2 points`

a) Sister Sledge
b) the Pointer Sisters
c) the Supremes
d) the Three Degrees

96. Diana Ross sang: "Reach out and touch somebody's hand/Make this world a better place, if you can." Who wrote the song? `2 points`

a) Smokey Robinson and Berry Gordy
b) Gamble and Huff
c) Ashford and Simpson
d) Womack and Womack

MORE GENERAL INTEREST

97. Which sitcom star had a 1975 hit with "When You're Young and in Love"?

a) Ja'Net DuBois
b) Ralph Carter
c) Tim Reid
d) Danielle Spencer

SCOTT'S #**5** PICK
FOR BEST ALBUMS OF
THE 1970s:

Let's Get It On, *Marvin Gaye* (1973)

Of course, in the far more permissive time hence, this album might be called Let's F***. *But Mr. Gaye wrote and recorded when audiences had as much imagination as the artists they worshipped—and Mr. Gaye gave it to us lovely. Fall in love to it or just screw your brains out: It's a soundtrack to a love affair that got stuck in lust mode.*

***Essential track:* "Distant Lover."**

[Answers on page 53]

What's Your HI-FI Q?

98. In which 1975 song did Natalie Cole describe her relationship as being "like words to a melody of love"? `2 points`

a) "Inseparable"
b) "I've Got Love on My Mind"
c) "Mr. Medley"
d) "This Will Be"

99. Which Ike and Tina Turner hit did the Supremes remake with the Four Tops in 1970? `2 points`

a) "River Deep—Mountain High"
b) "Proud Mary"
c) "Nutbush City Limits"
d) "A Fool in Love"

100. Whose background group, Love Unlimited, included his wife Glodean James as a member? `2 points`

a) Smokey Robinson
b) Grover Washington
c) Barry White
d) Bill Withers

101. In 1974, Rufus recorded "Stop On By" on *Rufusized*. Who originally wrote and performed this soul classic? `2 points`

a) Curtis Mayfield
b) Al Green
c) George Benson
d) Bobby Womack

102. Who wrote the score for the miniseries *Roots*? `2 points`

a) Isaac Hayes
b) Quincy Jones
c) Stevie Wonder
d) Maurice White

SCOTT'S #**3** PICK FOR BEST SINGLES OF THE 1970s:

"I'm Every Woman,"
Chaka Khan (1978)

What is there to say? The song that showed off all of Chaka's versatility and dazzle in four minutes of polished, ebullient, God-fearing R&B.

103. Which female group sang these lyrics in 1979: "You gonna make me love somebody else/If you keep on treatin' me the way you do"? `2 points`

a) the Jones Girls
b) the Debs
c) Sister Sledge
d) A Taste of Honey

104. Which Oscar-winning actor is the child of a vocalist in the Main Ingredient? `2 points`

a) Denzel Washington
b) Lou Gossett, Jr.
c) Whoopi Goldberg
d) Cuba Gooding, Jr.

105. Which funky seventies balladeer appeared on Broadway in *Your Arms Too Short to Box With God*? `2 points`

a) Al Green
b) Donny Hathaway
c) Lou Rawls
d) Barry White

106. Who wrote the classic "You Are So Beautiful" as a B side to one of his own singles before it became a hit for Joe Cocker? `2 points`

a) Billy Preston
b) Ray Charles
c) Ronald Isley
d) James Brown

107. According to the Five Stairsteps, things are "gonna get easier" and things are also "gonna get" what? `2 points`

a) tighter
b) brighter
c) whiter
d) slighter

SMOKEY'S #**3** PICK FOR
BEST SINGLES OF THE 1970s:

"The Payback,"
James Brown (1973)

Opening with a thumping bass line that laid the foundation for so many of hip-hop's club-heavy grooves, would you believe 30 seconds into the jam the drums announced the coming of something even funkier? "I'm mad!" the Godfather yells at his partner Fred Wesley. Oh, damn, now here comes the horns! Maybe this was, as the title suggests, JB's tale of revenge. "I can dig rappin'. . . I can dig scrappin', but I can't dig that backstabbing!" Crazy.

ASHFORD AND SIMPSON

108. Who recorded these three songs: "The Best of My Love," "Don't Go to Strangers," and "I Don't Wanna Lose Your Love"?
2 points

a) the Emotions
b) the Pointer Sisters
c) the Supremes
d) the Vandellas

109. Which Broadway musical introduced audiences to Melba Moore? **2 points**

a) *Purlie*
b) *Hair*
c) *The Wiz*
d) *Timbuktu*

110. Which songstress gained initial fame singing the lead on the Crusaders' 1979 classic "Street Life"? **2 points**

a) Rosie Gaines
b) Dee Dee Bridgewater
c) Brenda Russell
d) Randy Crawford

BONUS INTERNET QUESTION: Which Burt Reynolds urban action drama features "Street Life" as its theme song?

111. Who recorded these three songs: "I Don't Love You Anymore," "You Can't Hide From Yourself," and "The More I Get the More I Want"? **2 points**

a) Ronnie Dyson
b) Johnny Nash
c) Teddy Pendergrass
d) Al Green

SMOKEY'S #**5** PICK FOR
BEST ALBUMS OF THE 1970s:

Stand!, *Sly and the Family Stone (1969)*

Albeit released in 1969, this hit parade of an album would rock on well into the seventies, when the multiracial collective that was Sly and the Family Stone could do no wrong. With guitar-drenched hits like "I Want to Take You Higher" and "You Can Make It If You Try" leading the way, funk never had a more authentic run at the charts.

Essential tracks: *"Stand!" and "Everyday People."*

[Answers on page 53]

What's Your HI-FI Q?

SCOTT'S #**4** PICK FOR
BEST ALBUMS OF THE 1970s:

Ask Rufus, *Rufus featuring Chaka Khan* (1977)

Rufus's stew of jazz and funk brimmed with sonic clarity, never muddling the message in the music. Chaka Khan personified the inextricably intense way that a vocal line can become the song itself. Her range of sound became the song's range of emotion, taking you as high as you needed to get and as low as you tended to be. "Magic in Your Eyes" and "Everlasting Love" might be, frankly, the sexiest songs of the seventies, a two-fisted sequel to the band's earlier, magnificent "Little Boy Blue"—both sad and rueful, yet joyous in their romanticism. Rufus gets points for not being afraid of ideas—"Egyptian Song" and "Earth Song," refashion the love song for the smart urban neurotic who still had a jones to dance.

Essential tracks: "Hollywood" and "Close the Door."

112. Who recorded these three songs: "Soft and Wet," "Why You Treat Me So Bad," and "Sexy Dancer"? `2 points`

    a) Roger
    b) Prince
    c) Club Nouveau
    d) Marvin Gaye

113. Who recorded these three songs: "Slide," "Just a Touch of Love," and "Watching You"? `2 points`

    a) Maze
    b) the Floaters
    c) the Ohio Players
    d) Slave

114. Who recorded these three songs: "Work to Do," "Fight the Power," and "For the Love of You"? `2 points`

    a) the Dramatics
    b) the Impressions
    c) the Isley Brothers
    d) the Chi-Lites

BONUS INTERNET QUESTION: Name the artists who did covers of these songs.

115. Which soundtrack features these three Gladys Knight and the Pips songs: "On and On," "Make Yours a Happy Home," and "Mr. Welfare Man"? `2 points`

    a) *Claudine*
    b) *A Hero Ain't Nuttin' but a Sandwich*
    c) *Cornbread, Earl and Me*
    d) *Aaron Loves Angela*

116. Who recorded these three songs: "Thank You For Talkin' to Me, Africa," "Family Affair," and "Babies Makin' Babies"? `2 points`

a) Graham Central Station
b) Sly and the Family Stone
c) the Isley Brothers
d) Funkadelic

117. Minnie Riperton's 1974 debut album *Perfect Angel* was coproduced by which artist? `2 points`

a) Stevie Wonder
b) Lionel Richie
c) James Brown
d) Michael Jackson

118. Grandmaster Flash, Prince, and Michael Jackson were all born in what year? `2 points`

a) 1957
b) 1958
c) 1959
d) 1960

119. Which female group entertained during a bar scene in *The French Connection*? `2 points`

a) the Supremes
b) Honey Cone
c) A Taste of Honey
d) the Three Degrees

120. Which 1973 blaxploitation flick featured a soundtrack by jazz/R&B/fusion legend Roy Ayers? `2 points`

a) *Cleopatra Jones*
b) *Sheba Baby*
c) *Coffy*
d) *Foxy Brown*

SMOKEY'S #4 PICK FOR BEST ALBUMS OF THE 1970s:

Off the Wall, *Michael Jackson* (1979)

Take your pick: Was it Quincy Jones's pop masterpiece, or Michael Jackson's finest hour? Or both? Everything was there: the delicious grooves, the rocking dance tracks, the tear-filled ballads. It would be the last time Michael would just let his voice make the song. Perhaps MJ's illuminated socks on the album's front cover warned of more distracting things to come.

Essential tracks: "Rock With You" and "Don't Stop 'Til You Get Enough."

[Answers on page 53]

PATTI LABELLE

121. "Lady Marmalade," "Love Rollercoaster," and "Shining Star" all went to Number One on the charts in what year? [2 points]

a) 1975
b) 1976
c) 1977
d) 1978

122. "Found a Cure" was a huge hit in 1979 for which singing-songwriting duo? [2 points]

a) Ashford and Simpson
b) Womack and Womack
c) Rene and Angela
d) Yarbrough and Peoples

123. Before Bootsy Collins became part of the Parliament set, his Ohio-based band backed which funk-soul legend? [2 points]

a) James Brown
b) Otis Redding
c) Curtis Mayfield
d) Sly Stone

124. Which dance was made famous with a Van McCoy disco song? [2 points]

a) the Bus Stop
b) the Hustle
c) the Bump
d) the Freak

125. Which disco-era group had their first chart single with a remake of an old Judy Garland song called "Zing! Went the Strings of My Heart"? [2 points]

a) the Trammps
b) Rose Royce
c) MFSB
d) McFadden and Whitehead

[Answers on page 53]

SCOTT'S #2 PICK FOR BEST SINGLES OF THE 1970s:

"Street Life," the Crusaders (1979)

The R&B-tinged jazz ensemble made some of the silkiest jams of the seventies, mixing funk and jazz and blues into the mix, and dropping their sound right in the "pocket" every time. But it was with guest vocalist Randy Crawford that they achieved one of their greatest peaks. Crawford's dazzlingly distinctive vocal style provided the band with a lead instrument that gripped the ear and the mind, giving the honest and street-smart lyric an edge that stays with you long after a listen.

What's Your HI-FI Q?

126. Which singer had a 1978 hit called "Heaven Must Have Sent You" after going solo from her family group? `2 points`

a) June Pointer
b) Kathy Sledge
c) Bonnie Pointer
d) Anita Pointer

127. Which R&B diva got her start on *The Gong Show?* `2 points`

a) Cheryl Lynn
b) Thelma Houston
c) Martha Wash
d) Evelyn "Champagne" King

128. Bobby DeBarge left which Jermaine Jackson-discovered group to join the family group that bore his name? `2 points`

a) Switch
b) Ready for the World
c) Atlantic Starr
d) Slave

129. The Stone City Band was the backing group for which Motown musician? `2 points`

a) Rockwell
b) Marvin Gaye
c) Rick James
d) Lionel Richie

130. With which pop star did Donna Summer duet with on "No More Tears (Enough Is Enough)"? `2 points`

a) Olivia Newton-John
b) Barbra Streisand
c) Juice Newton
d) Debby Boone

131. In the Commodores' song, the narrator is "easy like" what?

a) morning coffee
b) Sunday morning
c) love and marriage
d) summer solstice

132. Which group was originally called the Big Apple Band? `5 points`

a) First Choice
b) the Sugar Hill Gang
c) the Village People
d) Chic

133. Which Loleatta Holloway hit was sampled in Marky Mark's "Good Vibrations"? `2 points`

a) "Hit and Run"
b) "Runaway"
c) "Love Sensation"
d) "Worn Out Broken Heart"

134. Which Kool & the Gang hit was the first to feature J.T. Taylor singing lead vocals? `2 points`

a) "Ladies Night"
b) "Too Hot"
c) "Celebration"
d) "Get Down on It"

135. Which singer won "The Amateur Hour" talent contest six weeks straight at New York's famed Apollo Theatre when she was nine years old? `2 points`

a) Stacy Lattisaw
b) Stephanie Mills
c) Teena Marie
d) Roberta Flack

SMOKEY'S #**3** PICK FOR
BEST ALBUMS OF THE 1970s:

**One Nation Under a Groove,
Funkadelic (1978)**

Flying from rock to jazz to soul and back again without ever losing any of the underlying funk, George Clinton and his crew (keyboardist Bernie Worrell, bassist/drummer Bootsy Collins, guitarist Michael Hampton, vocalist Junie Morrison et al.) created an orchestra of sound which still boggles the (maggot) brain. Funkadelic's music often spoke a different language, but when it could be understood—and not just heard—the results were ridiculously satisfying.

***Essential tracks:
"Grooveallegiance" and
"Who Says a Funk Band Can't Play Rock?"***

[Answers on page 53]

MILLIE JACKSON

136. Stephanie Mills was once married to which pop-soul group member? `2 points`

a) Shalamar's Howard Hewett
b) Shalamar's Jeffrey Daniels
c) the Sylvers' Leon Sylvers
d) the Jackson 5's Jermaine Jackson

137. Which group's debut album was actually the soundtrack to the movie *Car Wash*? `2 points`

a) Kool & the Gang
b) the Trammps
c) Rose Royce
d) the S.O.S. Band

138. Which artist left the Impressions two years before he released the soundtrack to *Superfly*?

a) Teddy Pendergrass
b) Curtis Mayfield
c) Al Green
d) Isaac Hayes

139. After leaving Motown Records in 1974, for which record label did the Jackson 5 record? `2 points`

a) Columbia Records
b) Atlantic Records
c) Blue Note Records
d) Epic Records

140. In 1972, Smokey Robinson left which group for a solo career? `2 points`

a) the Four Tops
b) the Soul Stirrers
c) the Blue Notes
d) the Miracles

[Answers on page 53]

SMOKEY'S **#2** PICK FOR

BEST SINGLES OF THE 1970s:

"I Miss You," Harold Melvin and the Blue Notes (1972)

If only every man could have the Blue Notes with him when it was time to apologize. This ultimate narrative of a black man's struggle to make up with his woman laid it all on the line. Featuring a gorgeous doo-wop chorus and the kind of moans and hollers that would be so often imitated in the years to come, it was Teddy P's growling smoothness ("down on my hands and knees, begging you please") that stole the show, and probably got him his girl back. Urban melodrama at its finest.

JAMES BROWN

141. Which song begins, "A boy is born in hard-town Mississippi"?
     5 points

     a) "Papa Was a Rolling Stone"
     b) "All I Do"
     c) "Inner City Blues"
     d) "Living for the City"

142. In 1973, James Brown produced which blaxploitation soundtrack? 5 points

     a) *Black Caesar*
     b) *Shaft*
     c) *Coffy*
     d) *Truck Turner*

143. Isaac Hayes's instrumental jam "Pursuit of the Pimpmobile" originally appeared on which soundtrack? 5 points

     a) *Shaft*
     b) *Foxy Brown*
     c) *Truck Turner*
     d) *Black Caesar*

144. Which of the following musicians was NOT a member of Funkadelic? 5 points

     a) Philip Bailey
     b) Bootsy Collins
     c) Bernie Worrell
     d) Junie Morrison

145. Who was "Kool" of Kool & the Gang? 5 points

     a) J.T. Taylor
     b) Robert Bell
     c) Ronald Bell
     d) George Clinton

[Answers on page 53]

SCOTT'S #2 PICK FOR BEST ALBUMS OF THE 1970s:

Off the Wall, *Michael Jackson* (1979)

We all knew MJ could sing like an angel, but this is where he found his voice. Aided and abetted by the master producer/arranger Quincy Jones, MJ brought a disco edge to pop and R&B that combined clubland electricity with smooth soul. Top-notch songwriters—Stevie Wonder, Paul McCartney, Rod Temperton among them—provided MJ with his best material since the early days at Motown, and he blessed them with the sweetest vocal sound this side of "I'll Be There." Coy and supple, raw and smooth, urgent yet laid back, his voice is the album's best instrument.

Essential tracks: "Rock With You" and "Off the Wall."

146. What disco song talks about "funky sounds wall-to-wall" with people "bumpin' booties, havin' us a ball, y'all"? **5 points**
    a) "Put Your Body in It"
    b) "Shake Your Body (Down to the Ground)"
    c) "Shake Your Groove Thing"
    d) "Dance, Dance, Dance (Yowsah, Yowsah, Yowsah)"

147. According to the 1976 Jacksons' hit, "don't blame it on the sunshine" or the "moonlight" or the "good times"; blame it on the what? **5 points**
    a) bad lies
    b) boogie
    c) lady
    d) love

148. Which Marvin Gaye album cover features Ernie Barnes's *Sugar Shack* painting—also known as the *Good Times* painting? **5 points**
    a) *What's Going On*
    b) *Here My Dear*
    c) *I Want You*
    d) *Distant Lover*

149. Who told us in "Thin Line Between Love and Hate" that "the sweetest woman in the world can be the meanest woman in the world"? **5 points**
    a) the Impressions
    b) the Persuaders
    c) the Chi-Lites
    d) the Four Tops

150. Which vocal group accompanies Donna Summer on "Heaven Knows"? **5 points**
    a) Brooklyn Dreams
    b) the Spinners
    c) the Temptations
    d) the Emotions

THE BEST SINGLE OF THE 1970s
ACCORDING TO SCOTT

"Harvest for the World," Isley Brothers (1976)

*Self-assured black folks' music at its best. Celebratory, anthemic—
the usual strong songwriting and dazzling vocals the Isleys are good for.*

Honorable Mention:

*"Don't Play That Song," Aretha Franklin (1970) • "I'll Be Around," the Spinners (1972) •
"Up the Ladder to the Roof," the Supremes (1970) • "O-o-h Child," the Five Stairsteps
(1970) • "(Not Just) Knee Deep (Pts I & II)," Funkadelic (1979)*

THE BEST SINGLE OF THE 1970s
ACCORDING TO SMOKEY

"I Will Survive," Gloria Gaynor (1979)

*"At first I was afraid, I was petrified . . ." So goes the most memorable first line in all of
music. If the seventies were about anthems, then Gloria Gaynor led the march with this
eight-minute burner that wouldn't still be a crowd-pleaser 20 years later without its fierce
rhythm section or its powerful message.*

Honorable Mention:

*"The Bottle," Gil Scott-Heron (1974) • "We Are Family," Sister Sledge (1979) • "It's Ecstasy
When You Lay Down Next to Me," Barry White (1977) • "Jungle Boogie," Kool & the Gang
(1974) • "You & I," Rick James (1978) • "Love Hangover," Diana Ross (1976) • "Love and
Happiness," Al Green (1972) • "I'll Be Around," the Spinners (1972) • "Running Away,"
Roy Ayers (1977) • "Le Freak," Chic (1978)*

STEVIE WONDER

THE BEST ALBUM OF THE 1970s ACCORDING TO SCOTT

Innervisions, *Stevie Wonder (1973)*

Stevie Wonder is the Master, and this is the Master's masterpiece. Stevie was the local boy with the global point of view, wedding the virtues of soul simplicity to pop pleasures, caressing the inner ear with a sense of melody that transcended any music-biz label: Was he a sensitive seventies singer/songwriter? Was he an R&B funkateer? Was he a sensual balladeer?

He was all of the above and then some. He might be, with Lennon-McCartney, one of the most covered songwriters in the modern pop landscape, because his songs delve deeper than they should and rise higher than we knew they could. No one else can write love songs and protest songs, narrative tales and stream-of-consciousness poems, with the same sense of wonder and craft; sometimes all in the same track (listen to "Jesus Children of America"). He is the fount from which all modern black music bubbles.

Essential tracks: *"Golden Lady" and "He's Misstra Know-It-All."*

THE BEST ALBUM OF THE 1970s ACCORDING TO SMOKEY

Songs in the Key of Life, *Stevie Wonder (1976)*

With two classic albums already under his belt, Wonder's more jazz-influenced tour de force brimmed with the poet's contagious optimism. From the opening hymn of "Have a Talk With God" to the heartfelt musings of "If It's Magic"; from the rolling bass line of "I Wish" to the swinging climactic energy that made "As" the staple of any good house party, Songs in the Key of Life had it all.

Essential tracks: *"Sir Duke" and "Pastime Paradise."*

What's Your HI-FI Q?

Give yourself one point for each correct answer, unless otherwise indicated. You can find answers to the Bonus Internet Questions at www.hifiq.com and www.blackbookscentral.com.

GENERAL INTEREST
1. b
2. c
3. b
4. c
5. b
6. b
7. b
8. c
9. b
10. a
11. b
12. d
13. c
14. d
15. c
16. b
17. b
18. c
19. b
20. c
21. c
22. a
23. b
24. b
25. b (2 points)
26. a
27. b (2 points)

28. b (2 points)
29. c
30. a (2 points)
31. b (2 points)
32. b (2 points)
33. a (2 points)
34. b (2 points)
35. c (2 points)
36. d (2 points)

LYRICALLY SPEAKING
37. a
38. c
39. b
40. c
41. b
42. d
43. b
44. b
45. b
46. c
47. c
48. c
49. a
50. a
51. b
52. b
53. a (2 points)

54. c (2 points)
55. b (2 points)
56. b (2 points)
57. b (2 points)
58. d (2 points)

LIGHTS, CAMERA, SOUNDTRACK
59. c
60. b
61. b
62. b
63. b (2 points)
64. a (2 points)
65. b (2 points)

COMPARE AND CONTRAST (ANALOGIES)
66. b. These are their first movies.
67. c. Both women were the lead singer of their respective groups.
68. d
69. b
70. d. Husband-and-wife singers each had "rocking" hit records.

71. a. Stevie and Rick each wrote those groups' breakout singles.
72. c. Both are covers of songs written by Paul Simon of Simon and Garfunkel.
73. b. Both songs are remakes of other hits. (2 points)

"AND NOW I'D LIKE TO INTRODUCE THE BAND . . ."
74. a
75. c
76. b
77. b
78. b
79. a (2 points)
80. a (2 points)
81. b (2 points)
82. b (2 points)
83. b (2 points)
84. d (2 points)
85. a (2 points)
86. b (2 points)
87. a (2 points)

THEY WRITE THE SONGS (SONGWRITING)
88. a
89. b
90. b
91. b
92. a

93. b
94. a (2 points)
95. b (2 points)
96. c (2 points)

MORE GENERAL INTEREST
97. b
98. a (2 points)
99. a (2 points)
100. c (2 points)
101. d (2 points)
102. b (2 points)
103. a (2 points)
104. d (2 points)
105. a (2 points)
106. a (2 points)
107. b (2 points)
108. a (2 points)
109. b (2 points)
110. d (2 points)
111. c (2 points)
112. b (2 points)
113. d (2 points)
114. c (2 points)
115. a (2 points)
116. b (2 points)
117. a (2 points)
118. b (2 points)
119. d (2 points)
120. c (2 points)
121. a (2 points)
122. a (2 points)
123. a (2 points)

124. b (2 points)
125. a (2 points)
126. c (2 points)
127. a (2 points)
128. a (2 points)
129. c (2 points)
130. b (2 points)
131. b
132. d (5 points)
133. c (2 points)
134. a (2 points)
135. b (2 points)
136. b (2 points)
137. c (2 points)
138. b
139. d (2 points)
140. d (2 points)
141. d (5 points)
142. a (5 points)
143. c (5 points)
144. a (5 points)
145. b (5 points)
146. c (5 points)
147. b (5 points)
148. c (5 points)
149. b (5 points)
150. a (5 points)

TOTAL POSSIBLE SCORE: 266 points

ENTER YOUR SCORE HERE

Answers

Press Pause

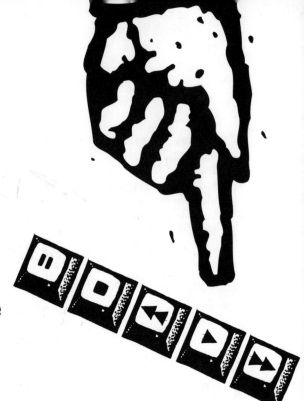

THE FIVE BEST BLUE-EYED SOUL RECORDS OR, PLAY THAT FUNKY MUSIC, WHITE BOY

1. "Square Biz," Teena Marie (1981)

We all thought she was a light-skinned black girl when she hit the scene, because no white girl could blow like that and still be a white girl, right? Teena Marie changed all that. Swooping and hollering, shouting and crooning, Teena Marie's vocal style was undeniably steeped in the rhythms of the (rhythm &) blues and early rap, but it was all her own, as were, primarily, the words she sang. Granted this slot could be filled with "Casanova Brown" or "Lover Girl" or "Behind the Groove" or "Sucker for Your Love" or "Ooo La La La" or . . . well, you get the point. The only reason "Square Biz" ranks number one, is that you gotta respect a white girl who name-checks Maya Angelou and Nikki Giovanni in the process.

2. "I Can't Go For That (No Can Do)" Daryl Hall and John Oates (1981)

When this record came out back in the day, nobody in our neighborhood knew these were the same guys who'd made "Private Eyes" and "Kiss on My List." Percolating with a paranoid percussiveness and a loping beat that stayed just behind the groove, this song managed to be both hot and cool, a love song with an edge. Daryl Hall's lead vocals dotted the track with the kind of sexy assertiveness you find in some of Marvin Gaye's sly moments. And it had enough mystery—what, exactly, was the "that" he couldn't go for?—to make it withstand the test of time.

3. Colour by Numbers, Culture Club (1983)

Boy George never gets the credit he deserves as one of the finest singer/songwriters to come out of that British Invasion that made the early eighties such a vivid and exciting time for music. Sure, the stuff on Culture Club's debut, Kissing to Be Clever, was entertaining and bouncily fun, but Colour By Numbers was a brilliant soul-flavored follow-up—and not simply because of the Motown- and Solar-inspired singles like "Karma Chameleon" and "It's a Miracle" that climbed the pop charts. Check out Boy George's crooning on such polished ballads

55

What's Your HI-FI Q?

as "Victims" and "That's the Way (I'm Only Trying to Help You)." Often backed by the soul-shouting pyrotechnics of Helen Terry and the merest hint of piano, Boy dipped and dived through terrific melodies, sussing out the soul with a coy blend of confidence and pathos that makes the heart break.

4. "Lowdown," Boz Scaggs (1976)

Scaggs indulged in his love of soul music on several albums; but none of his singles achieved the kind of sly, soul symbiosis of "Lowdown." Mixing a cynically dry tone with a supple, deep groove sound, Scaggs created an anthem of seventies nastiness that still managed to have a heart. With his sexy baritone and gift for arch turns of phrase that never seemed to force the issue, Boz Scaggs was a critic's darling who also found a huge audience. "Lowdown," one of the finest moments of seventies pop music, is a classic of jive talkin' loveliness.

5. TIE—"Young Americans," David Bowie (1975); "Everybody," Madonna (1983)

Why? Because Bowie knew that Philly soul was the new "Sound of Young America" and wore it like a second skin. Because Bowie used Luther Vandross on the background of all that great music. Because he was fierce enough to turn out Soul Train. Because to say what he had to say about America, he knew that a black sound was the only true sound there was. And finally, because of one of the best lyrics in the history of pop music: "Ain't there one damn song that can make me break down and cry?" Yes, it's called "Young Americans," David. Why the two of them together? Because Bowie is the real reason there is a Madonna, another shape-shifter who dabbled in everything along the way, more to keep herself interested in the pop game than anything else. Because her first album rocked the urban world harder than it rocked the pop one. Because she's a thief who knows to steal from the best—whether she's trying on Latin culture or voguing with the gay boys—yet has still managed to have her own point of view. Because the sheer level of her confidence made up for the almost-there voice. But mostly because she knew, and still knows, how to get the party started.

Honorable Mention:

"Higher Love," Steve Winwood (1986)
"Everything She Wants," Wham! (1985)
"All Around the World," Lisa Stansfield (1990)
"Groove Is in the Heart," Deee-Lite (1990)
"You Should Be Dancing," Bee Gees (1976)

THE FIVE BEST DUETS

1. "The Closer I Get to You," Roberta Flack with Donny Hathaway (1978)

We could have chosen the entire duets album they made in 1972, with the beautiful "Be Real Black for Me" and the original "I (Who Have Nothing)" and "Where Is the Love." And we could have chosen the second duet album they did, which includes the incomparable "Back Together Again." But we chose this cut, simply because Donny is at his most passionate. The song has a sturdiness that makes it a true classic, and it's on Roberta's fabulous Ahmet Ertegun–produced Blue Lights in the Basement album. Damn, these voices blend so well, like they were born to sing together, dripping with a sweetness that never congealed into saccharine falseness, and an easygoing, honest approach to the music that allowed them to just sing the notes, tell the story, and make the song itself live. Truly astonishing artistry.

2. "Saturday Love," Cherrelle with Alexander O'Neal (1986)

This should almost be considered a quartet rather than a duet, because the writing/production team behind it, Jimmy Jam and Terry Lewis, created the sonic lushness which backed the singers with such distinct personality that they seem as integral to the record as the singers do. Alexander O'Neal's voice is a wonder to behold, a gutsy, golden instrument that might have been the truest on radio in the eighties. Cherrelle's vocals complement him expertly; feminine in a way singers aren't feminine anymore—but in a good way, sleek, sexy, and polished to a high gloss that never attempted more than it should have. This song's simplicity was the key to its success. The singers made it a universal ode to romance, both danceable and chillable, a sly mix of cool passion and hot lust. "Saturday Love" represents the beginning of a beautiful musical relationship.

3. "Baby, I'm Scared of You," Womack and Womack (1983)

Maybe the bloodlines say it all: He's one of the gospel-singing Womacks, she's the daughter of fifties genius Sam Cooke. How could they go wrong? They couldn't and they don't on this stylish, smart, devastatingly spirited ode to marriage, love, and the games people play in the midst of such states. From its suave, loping beat to its perfectly blended points of view, this song stood out in the eighties because it stressed intelligence rather than just raw passion. This was the thinking folks' love duet.

What's Your
HI-FI Q?

4. "Fire and Desire," Rick James and Teena Marie (1981)

Raw sex on a platter. Rick James at the top of his form. Teena Marie hitting the vocal nail right on its head. This was grown-folks music in the most intimate way. Rising and falling like a humping couple under a sweaty sheet, you'd be surprised if it didn't melt on your turntable. Rick's spoken-word intro raised the stakes for brothers everywhere, managing to be both slick and vulnerable (but never sleazy, that would come later for Rick)—maybe his finest moment. Teena brought out the best in him.

5. "I'll Be There for You/You're All I Need to Get By," Method Man featuring Mary J. Blige (1995)

Hip-hop was waiting for something like this—and so was the world, based on the way this hit blew up the summer of 1995. Based on the Motown hits "I'll Be There for You" and "You're All I Need to Get By," this cut was thug love at its hip-hop hottest, blending Meth's slacker rawness with Mary's drama-queen passion, and then frothing it into an anthem of young love that transcended its ghetto realism simply because it was so site specific. Talk about keeping it real: "My lady, we can make war or make babies." Succinct and to the point. Never coy, always honest. Maybe this is how Marvin would spit it if he was still here.

Honorable Mention:

"If This World Were Mine," Luther Vandross and Cheryl Lynn (1982)
"Two Hearts," Stephanie Mills and Teddy Pendergrass (1981)
"Don't Look Any Further," Dennis Edwards and Siedah Garrett (1984)
"How Do You Keep the Music Playing," James Ingram and Patti Austin (1983)
"My Mistake (Was to Love You)," Diana Ross and Marvin Gaye (1974)

Press Play

WHITNEY AND MICHAEL

THE 80s

R&B Goes Pop

What's Your HI-FI Q?

THE EIGHTIES: R&B GOES POP

The Eighties . . . the decade that gave birth to MTV; when "video killed the radio star"; when disco died; when R&B aimed for crossover; when a black child star from the seventies matured into the biggest act in pop music.

New Jack Swing swung us around dance floors as producers became a force in black music. Teddy Riley led the pack alongside Jimmy Jam and Terry Lewis and Quincy Jones, the jazzman who brought his ace arranging skills to an R&B scene that was about to "beat it" to the highest levels it could reach.

Who knew when Michael Jackson released a Lite-FM duet with Paul McCartney that he was only previewing what would eventually become the biggest solo album of all time, the album that would pave the way for a series of multi-hit albums and Top 10 hits, for video dominance, and for black music becoming the music of the marketed masses?

Who knew that a skinny kid from Minneapolis who called himself Prince would challenge Michael Jackson for pop-star dominance, stalking about on high heels, foreseeing the eighties return to androgyny, mixing rock guitar with funk rhythms, while becoming a movie star in the process?

Who knew that Michael's little sister, heretofore known for a camera-savvy Mae West impression and years of TV work, would strike a pose of independence so fierce that fans the world over would launch her into a stardom that could only be rivaled by her brother? Ms. Jackson, indeed.

And who knew that thing we called rap music would infiltrate the airwaves, come out of the 'hood, creep into the suburbs, and duet with Aerosmith?

You didn't have to watch *Dynasty* to have an attitude, but it helped. It wasn't just about who shot J.R. but why did somebody shoot Marvin? We lost Scott LaRock, but we got edutained by KRS-One. Disco wasn't really dead, it was just becoming something called "house," though the kids in Chi-Town knew that all along. Your Uzi weighed a ton, Luther was the new loverman, Lionel Richie was dancing on the ceiling, and Big Brother didn't matter because Slave was watching you.

What do you think about the eighties?

Answer some of these questions and see if you can remember the time.

What's Your HI-FI Q?

1.   Which artist officially added an exclamation point to the end of his name?

a) Al B. Sure
b) Prince
c) Puff Daddy
d) M.C. Hammer

2.   Which Jackson sibling NEVER released a solo album?

a) Rebbie Jackson
b) Jackie Jackson
c) La Toya Jackson
d) Jermaine Jackson

3.   Pebbles is the cousin of which R&B star?

a) Karyn White
b) Toni Braxton
c) Cherrelle
d) Oleta Adams

4.   Whose debut album presented itself as "Introducing the Hardline According to . . ."?

a) Jermaine Stewart
b) Eddy Grant
c) Terence Trent D'Arby
d) Larry Blackmon

5.   Who sang "Heartbeat" in 1981?

a) La Toya Jackson
b) Taana Gardner
c) Lisa Lisa
d) Stephanie Mills

SCOTT'S #**10** PICK FOR
BEST SINGLES OF THE 1980s:

"So Watcha Sayin'," EPMD (1989)

Clean and crisp, yet still brimming with flavor. The rhythms of rap should always have this track's suppleness.

6. Which artist remade Prince's "Do Me, Baby"?

a) Angela Winbush
b) Me'lisa Morgan
c) Grace Jones
d) Chaka Khan

7. In 1985, what faux-military man scored a monster international hit with the album *Trapped*?

a) Peabo Bryson
b) Capt. Kangaroo
c) Colonel Abrams
d) Johnny "Guitar" Watson

8. What kind of animal is Michael Jackson holding on the inside of the *Thriller* album?

a) parakeet
b) monkey
c) baby tiger
d) lizard

9. MC Lyte's brother Milk was chillin' on which 1988 hip-hop classic?

a) "The Bridge Is Over"
b) "Top Billin'"
c) "Eric B. Is President"
d) "Rapper's Delight"

10. Which present-day preacher was once known as the "Son of Kurtis Blow"?

a) Russell Simmons
b) DJ Run
c) M.C. Hammer
d) Mase

SMOKEY'S #**10** PICK FOR BEST SINGLES OF THE 1980s:

"Roxanne, Roxanne,"
U.T.F.O. (1984)

It started off innocently enough, but talk about genre-creating: For over a year, this international Number One hit spawned hundreds of "answer" records, all focused on the encounter between a hot girl and a group of, well, wack guys. But Mixmaster Ice, the Kangol Kid, Dr. Ice, and the Educated Rapper actually got dissed for having high IQs—guess you do need a Benz.

[Answers on page 130]

65

BOBBY BROWN

11. **What singer of the 1988 hit "Girlfriend" was once married to one of the cofounders of LaFace Records?**

a) Chili
b) Beyoncé Knowles
c) Chanté Moore
d) Pebbles

12. **Who performed the 1984 *Billboard* #1 hit single "Oh Sheila"?**

a) Hi-Five
b) Ready for the World
c) Club Nouveau
d) Digital Underground

13. **Bobby Brown appeared in how many of New Edition's seven studio albums?**

a) 7
b) 5
c) 3
d) 2

14. **In the late eighties, who turned polka-dot shirts into an urban style?**

a) Special Ed
b) Kwamé
c) Sir Mix-A-Lot
d) M.C. Hammer

15. **What was Afrika Bambaataa and Soulsonic Force's follow-up single to "Planet Rock"?**

a) "Play That Beat Mr. DJ"
b) "Looking for the Perfect Beat"
c) "Zulu Groove"
d) "Renegades of Funk"

SCOTT'S #**10** PICK FOR
BEST ALBUMS OF THE 1980s:

Raising Hell, *Run-DMC (1986)*

Their first album may have established them as keepers, but Raising Hell *confirmed them as legends. Careening from brand-name rock styling ("Walk This Way") to melodious storytelling ("Peter Piper"),* Hell *gave hip-hop a polished sheen on which to wax poetic. Here you'll find the cultural redefinition of what it means to be a "Rock Star."*

Essential track: "My Adidas."

[Answers on page 130]

THE FRESH PRINCE

16. What was the first hip-hop album to be certified platinum?
`2 points`

a) M.C. Hammer, *Please Hammer, Don't Hurt 'Em*
b) Public Enemy, *It Takes a Nation of Millions to Hold Us Back*
c) Beastie Boys, *Licensed to Ill*
d) D.J. Jazzy Jeff and the Fresh Prince, *He's the D.J., I'm the Rapper*

17. Which of these "Don't" songs came out third? `2 points`

a) "Don't You Worry 'Bout a Thing," by Stevie Wonder
b) "Don't Stop 'Til You Get Enough," by Michael Jackson
c) "Don't Be Cruel," by Bobby Brown
d) "Don't Let Go (Love)," by En Vogue

18. Who recorded the original version of "Get Here"? `2 points`

a) Brenda Russell
b) Oleta Adams
c) Dionne Warwick
d) Karyn White

19. What eighties hit did Tevin Campbell remake? `2 points`

a) "Stomp!"
b) "Strawberry Letter 23"
c) "Solid"
d) "So Fine"

20. Who recorded the original version of "As We Lay"? `2 points`

a) Gwen Guthrie
b) Shirley Murdock
c) Minnie Riperton
d) Millie Jackson

SMOKEY'S **#10** PICK FOR
BEST ALBUMS OF THE 1980s:

Purple Rain, *Prince and the Revolution* (1984)

An obvious choice, but no less worthy. These nine songs have become so commonplace because they are simply that good. It was pop defined by an electric guitar, rock and roll interpreted by a genius of rhythm and blues. "When Doves Cry" defines the sound of the eighties better than any other single song, while "Let's Go Crazy" brought good disco feeling to what had been, up to then, a pretty dreary decade. "Dearly beloved, we are gathered here today to get through this thing called life." Yeah, you know the words.

Essential tracks: "Purple Rain," "Darling Nikki," and "The Beautiful Ones."

What's Your HI-FI Q?

21. Which British-born soul stirrer hit it big in 1988 with the song "Never Gonna Give You Up"? `2 points`

a) Jamiroquai
b) George Michael
c) Rick Astley
d) Lisa Stansfield

22. Which former *All My Children* star scored a Number One hit in 1986 for "Shake You Down"? `2 points`

a) Shemar Moore
b) Eddie Murphy
c) Billy Ocean
d) Gregory Abbott

23. The first Grammy awarded to a rap artist was in 1988 for which song? `2 points`

a) "Parents Just Don't Understand"
b) "I'll Be Missing You"
c) "Girls Are Nothing but Trouble"
d) "Gangsta's Paradise"

24. Bassist Bootsy Collins was known for wearing which geometric shape in his sunglasses? `2 points`

a) triangle
b) circle
c) star
d) square

25. What was the 1989 follow-up album to the Beastie Boys' 8X-platinum *Licensed To Ill* LP? `2 points`

a) *The Low End Theory*
b) *Paul's Boutique*
c) *It Was Written*
d) *Walking With a Panther*

SCOTT'S #**9** PICK FOR BEST SINGLES OF THE 1980s:

"Tell Me I'm Not Dreaming,"
Jermaine Jackson and Michael
Jackson (1984)

The prodigal brothers got together to record a top-notch single that never really saw the light of day. Find it and tell me it's not one of Michael's finest vocal moments.

26. In 1989, what late-night host's overweight "alter ego" signed a recording contract with MCA Records? **2 points**
   a) Keenan Ivory Wayans
   b) David Letterman
   c) Arsenio Hall
   d) Magic Johnson

27. On the album cover to Ice-T's 1988 *Power* LP, who was featured holding a shotgun? **2 points**
   a) President Ronald Reagan
   b) KRS-One
   c) Paris
   d) Darlene, his wife

28. This *Cosby Show* guest star once had it made by calling himself "the youngest in charge." **2 points**
   a) Shyheim
   b) Will Smith
   c) Heavy D
   d) Special Ed

29. Which song was released second? **2 points**
   a) "Adore," by Prince
   b) "Pray," by M.C. Hammer
   c) "Respect," by Aretha Franklin
   d) "Cherish," by Kool & the Gang

30. When the single "Purple Rain" entered the charts, which Prince and the Revolution hit was already at Number One? **2 points**
   a) "When Doves Cry"
   b) "Let's Go Crazy"
   c) "Baby I'm a Star"
   d) "Take Me With U"

[Answers on page 130]

SMOKEY'S #**9** PICK FOR
BEST SINGLES OF THE 1980s:

*"It Takes Two," Rob Base & D.J.
E-Z Rock (1988)*

Yeah, I know it's a sample and its rhyme probably stunted hip-hop's lyrical progress for a few summers, but there has been no better song to ever rock a dance floor. After you hear Slick Rick say "hit it," I defy you not to move your ass to this sweaty anthem. "I wanna rock right now." Thanks, James.

THE REAL ROXANNE

31. Which of the following is NOT the name of a "Roxanne, Roxanne" inspired single? `2 points`

a) "Roxanne's a Man"
b) "Roxanne's Mother"
c) "Roxanne's Comeback"
d) "The Real Roxanne"

32. Janet Jackson was 19 when she eloped with . . . `2 points`

a) Rene Elizondo
b) Chico DeBarge
c) James DeBarge
d) Taimak

33. Which supermodel gets the Prince treatment on 1988's *The Black Album*? `2 points`

a) Naomi Campbell
b) Cindy Crawford
c) Jerry Hall
d) Tyra Banks

34. Public Enemy's *It Takes a Nation of Millions to Hold Us Back* was introduced at what famous theater? `2 points`

a) the Apollo Theatre in Harlem
b) the Hammersmith Odeon in London
c) Ford's Theatre in Washington, D.C.
d) the Hammerstein Ballroom in N.Y.C.

35. Who wrote and sang the eighties ode to memories "Forget Me Nots"?

a) Angela Winbush
b) Patrice Rushen
c) Siedah Garrett
d) Bettye LaVette

SCOTT'S #**9** PICK FOR BEST ALBUMS OF THE 1980s:

Rapture, *Anita Baker (1986)*

Redefining the meaning of "lush." Anita Baker caught us up in the rapture of her velvet tones and songs of love, and made adult music popular again. So emotionally at the ready, it was like a big kiss to the world. The big, bawling "Sweet Love" was a bold moment for radio and jaded ears, crooning new life into a staple that hadn't had much life left in it: the well-written song. And that wasn't the only one: Rapture might be the most solid start-to-finish album of the decade, stuffed full of catchy melodies and tunes that stuck in the head, mostly because of Baker's soulful voice.

***Essential tracks:** "Same Ole Love" and "Mystery."*

[Answers on page 130]

GRANDMASTER FLASH

36. DJ Grandmaster Flash invented a way for two turntables to share the same sound output. What is this called? `2 points`

a) cross-fading
b) scratch-mixing
c) break-dancing
d) battling

37. Who opened for Public Enemy's first national tour in 1988? `2 points`

a) the Beastie Boys
b) X-Clan
c) Big Daddy Kane
d) L.L. Cool J

38. What was the original name of the *Sign 'O' the Times* LP? `5 points`

a) *Purple Passion*
b) *Crystal Ball*
c) *Time Heels All Wounds*
d) *The Black Album*

39. Which of these divas has won a Best Song Oscar at the Academy Awards as well as a 1984 Grammy for Best Inspirational Vocal? `5 points`

a) Donna Summer
b) Diana Ross
c) Dionne Warwick
d) Whitney Houston

40. Which song did Vanessa Williams sing in the talent section of the Miss America pageant? `5 points`

a) "A Natural Woman (You Make Me Feel Like)"
b) "Touch Me in the Morning"
c) "Lush Life"
d) "Happy Days Are Here Again"

[Answers on page 130]

SMOKEY'S #**9** PICK FOR
BEST ALBUMS OF THE 1980s:

Rapture, *Anita Baker* (1986)

When you have a voice that can move mountains, the music making should be easy. Or at least it should feel easy, and Ms. Baker's debut album came across as absolutely effortless. Jazz melodies abounded, but with a contemporary flair, while each song flowed with the vocal confidence that can only be displayed by a master of her craft.

Essential tracks: "Sweet Love" and "Been So Long."

ERIC B., RUSSELL SIMMONS,
L.L. COOL J

LYRICALLY SPEAKING

41. "Dig if you will the picture" is the first line of which hit song?

a) "When Doves Cry," by Prince
b) "Let's Go Crazy," by Prince
c) "All Cried Out," by Lisa Lisa and Cult Jam
d) "Let's All Chant," by Michael Zager

42. Which designer is "no friend of mine" in "Rock Box"?

a) Tommy Hilfiger
b) Calvin Klein
c) Sergio Valente
d) Sean John

43. What kind of bakery item does Rakim liken himself to in "Eric B. Is President"?

a) a muffin
b) a donut
c) a bagel
d) a piece of corn bread

44. The phrase "Hasta la Vista, Baby," was a tagline from which Jody Watley hit?

a) "Looking for a New Love"
b) "Still a Thrill"
c) "Don't You Want Me"
d) "Most of All"

45. In a 1984 Prince ballad, who "smash[es] the picture, always, every time"?

a) a woman scorned
b) the beautiful ones
c) the lovely ones
d) the girls next-door

[Answers on page 130]

What's Your HI-FI Q?

46. Which song starts: "Flash back—Who's that/Dancing to the latest"?

a) "Behind the Groove"
b) "Disco Nights"
c) "Party Train"
d) "Square Biz"

47. Which male group sang the lyrics "The sky is calm, the stars are bright/What's better than 2 be in flight"?

a) the Time
b) the Gap Band
c) Troop
d) New Edition

48. Which song includes the lyrics: "She saw him standing in the section marked/'If you have to ask, you can't afford it' lingerie"? `2 points`

a) "A Love Bizarre"
b) "Nasty Girl"
c) "The Glamorous Life"
d) "Sugar Walls"

49. Which seminal hip-hop jam opens with the query "Party people . . . do u wanna get funky"? `2 points`

a) "Do You Wanna Get Funky"
b) "Looking for the Perfect Beat"
c) "Rapper's Delight"
d) "Planet Rock"

50. In 1988, who warned men that she's " . . . not the kind of girl that you can let down and think that everything is okay"? `2 points`

a) Jody Watley
b) Karyn White
c) Patti LaBelle
d) Mariah Carey

SCOTT'S #**8** PICK FOR BEST SINGLES OF THE 1980s:

"Rock the Bells" L.L. Cool J (1985)

The intro to the hardest-working brother in hip-hop. An ego trip with all the trimmings. This is fundamental rap music for the ages.

51. In "Little Red Corvette," Prince exclaims the object of his affection must be a what? `2 points`

a) dream machine
b) limousine
c) Trans Am
d) BMW 330i

52. Which 1988 hip-hop party classic ends with the line " . . . 1, 2, 3, get loose now!"? `2 points`

a) "This Is How We Do It"
b) "It Takes Two"
c) "The Show"
d) "O.P.P."

53. Who was the first artist to intone " . . . the revolution will not be televised"? `2 points`

a) Chuck D
b) KRS-One
c) Gil Scott-Heron
d) Curtis Mayfield

54. In 1989, what three words introduced Q-Tip to listeners? `5 points`

a) "black is black"
b) "I love you"
c) "kiss my back"
d) "I love daisies"

55. After "Peter Piper picked peppers . . ." who "rocked rhymes"? `5 points`

a) DMC
b) L.L. Cool J
c) Run
d) Rakim

SMOKEY'S **#8** PICK FOR
BEST SINGLES OF THE 1980s:

"Top Billin'," Audio Two (1988)

If you had to reduce hip-hop music to its two core elements, you would get the hot beat and straight-ahead rhyme of "Top Billin'." "That's how it is/You can ask Giz/I stole your girl while you was in prison," Milk announced, over a drum line that has become an indelible part of the music's sonic vocabulary. Four years later, producers would slyly use it as the backbeat for Mary J. Blige's seminal hip-hop soul cut "Real Love."

RUN-DMC

56. In the song "Kiss," "you don't have to watch" what on TV "to have an attitude"? `2 points`

a) "Dallas"
b) "the time"
c) "Dynasty"
d) "me dance"

57. Which royal moniker should "sucker MCs" call Run in "King of Rock"? `2 points`

a) Duke
b) Prince
c) Sire
d) Mr.

58. In 1987's "I Know You Got Soul," what have you "slept through" while Rakim was away? `2 points`

a) "weak shows"
b) "wack rhymes"
c) "silly love songs"
d) "nightmares"

59. Which song ended with L.L. whispering "I'll be waiting . . . I'll love you"? `2 points`

a) "I Need Love"
b) "Around the Way Girl"
c) "Big Ole Butt"
d) "The Boomin' System"

60. In "Rock the Bells," L.L.'s not a virgin, so who can he "make scream"? `2 points`

a) Janet Jackson
b) Madonna
c) Samantha Fox
d) "all the pretty ladies"

SCOTT'S #8 PICK FOR BEST ALBUMS OF THE 1980s:

Control, *Janet Jackson* (1986)

If the Declaration of Independence had this kind of soul, we'd all be living in a rhythm nation. Jimmy Jam and Terry Lewis gave Janet a loving place to find herself—and found themselves in the process. Not that they hadn't created some jams before this; but with Janet on the mike, their sounds found a nation ready to let the rhythm hit 'em. The slinky grooves Jam and Lewis created were like a fairground full of open-all-night attractions where you could find love, pride, and most of all, fun.

***Essential tracks:** "When I Think of You" and "Pleasure Principle."*

[Answers on page 130]

SLICK RICK

61. In "Sign 'O' the Times" Prince believed that, "some say a man ain't happy truly" until what? **2 points**

a) "he truly flies"
b) "he truly dies"
c) "he sings a song"
d) "he gets some ass"

62. Who is the female protagonist of Slick Rick's "La-Di-Da-Di"? **2 points**

a) Sally
b) Michelle
c) Roxanne
d) Molly

63. In "La-Di-Da-Di," what time did Slick Rick wake up? **5 points**

a) 8:30 a.m.
b) 12:06 a.m.
c) 10:00 a.m.
d) 11:00 a.m.

64. What kind of cologne did Slick Rick use " . . . for all the girls he might take home"? **5 points**

a) Issey Miyake
b) Polo
c) Blue Jean
d) Drakkar

65. "Relax your minds, let your conscience be free, and get down to the sounds of . . ." whom? **2 points**

a) "Puff Daddy"
b) "EPMD"
c) "the great Fugees"
d) "me on the M-I-C"

SMOKEY'S #**8** PICK FOR
BEST ALBUMS OF THE 1980s:

Bad, *Michael Jackson (1987)*

We all know what Thriller *achieved, but* Bad *made MJ an international superstar—the likes of which the world had never seen. His lofty long-form videos for "Smooth Criminal," "Dirty Diana," and "The Way You Make Me Feel" aided in the hero worship, while "Man in the Mirror" made even the Jacko non-believers run to find a congregation. Quincy Jones's last great pop statement.*

Essential tracks: "Man in the Mirror" and "Bad."

[Answers on page 130]

What's Your HI-FI Q?

66. Who remade the DeBarge song that includes these lyrics: "I had some problems/And no one could seem to solve them"? `2 points`

a) Vesta Williams
b) Patti LaBelle
c) Regina Belle
d) Whitney Houston

67. Who sang the lyrics "You told me a lie and you didn't have an alibi/But baby, yet I still cared"? `2 points`

a) Cheryl Lynn
b) Gwen Guthrie
c) Jennifer Holliday
d) Jocelyn Brown

68. In 1987, which rapper declared that the "Bronx keeps creatin' it, and Queens keeps on fakin' it"? `2 points`

a) Chuck D
b) Big Pun
c) KRS-One
d) Snoop Doggy Dogg

69. In what 1985 song did Prince sing about "Old Man Johnson's farm"? `2 points`

a) "Kiss"
b) "Pop Life"
c) "Raspberry Beret"
d) "Take Me With U"

70. With whom did Prince sing "If we cannot make babies/Maybe we can make some time . . ." on his B-side classic "Erotic City"? `2 points`

a) Wendy Melvoin
b) Sheena Easton
c) Cat
d) Sheila E.

SCOTT'S #**7** PICK FOR BEST SINGLES OF THE 1980s:

"I Know You Got Soul," Eric B. & Rakim (1987)

The best rap performance of the eighties, if not ever. Rakim didn't have to shout to be heard. His smooth flow was like a sail on the ocean.

71. Which rap crew recorded a version of "Wipeout" with the Beach Boys in 1987?
   a) Whodini
   b) Run-DMC
   c) Heavy D. and the Boyz
   d) Fat Boys

72. The singer of 1989's "Love Under New Management" was also once in a group called Side Effect. Who is she?
   a) Linda Hopkins
   b) Stephanie Mills
   c) Miki Howard
   d) Nona Hendryx

73. Who demanded "Ronnie, Talk to Russia" on a 1981 album?
   a) Peabo Bryson
   b) Roger
   c) Morris Day
   d) Prince

74. Who sang the lyrics "Walking down the street/Watching ladies go by watching you"?
   a) Maze
   b) Madhouse
   c) Slave
   d) Craze

75. According to "Sign 'O' the Times,": "in September my cousin tried reefer for the very first time, now he's doin' horse, it's . . ." when? **2 points**
   a) ". . . fall"
   b) ". . . June"
   c) ". . . noon"
   d) ". . . doom"

[Answers on page 130]

SMOKEY'S #**7** PICK FOR
BEST SINGLES OF THE 1980s:

"Rock the Bells," L.L. Cool J (1985)

This testosterone-filled piece of old-school battle rap made a star out of a teenager. "Some girls will like this jam, and some girls won't/ 'Cause I make a lot of money and your boyfriend don't," L.L. boasted. With its ska-inspired backbeat, scratch-mix call-and-response inserts, and a punishing set of drops by the great DJ Cut Creator, it may be impossible for this hip-hop hall of famer to create a more head-banging record.

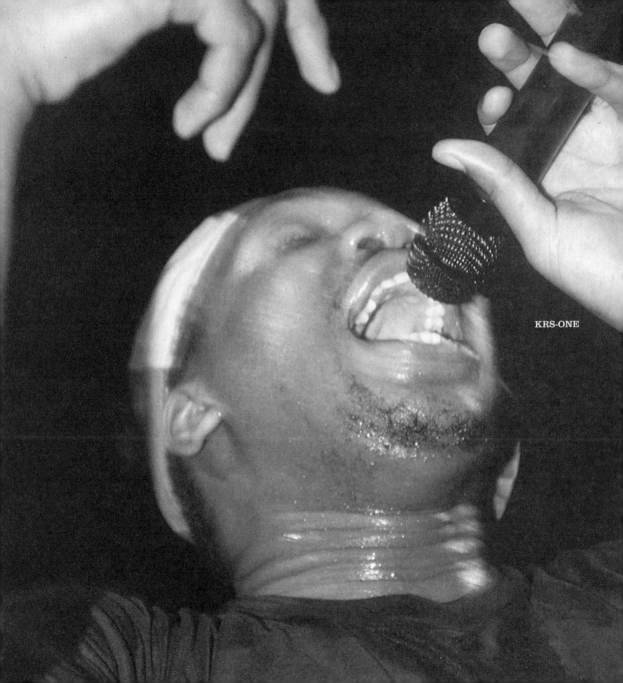

KRS-ONE

76. In 1987, who was "so fond of Honda Scooters" he "bought 74"? `2 points`

 a) Special Ed
 b) Heavy D
 c) Slick Rick
 d) Chubb Rock

77. KRS-One's "The Bridge Is Over" boast refers to what? `2 points`

 a) the Brooklyn Bridge falling down
 b) he would not use James Brown samples anymore
 c) Queensbridge, N.Y.'s reign on hip-hop was coming to an end
 d) the song's verse is coming back

78. " 'I don't love her'/I tried to tell myself" is the first line to which hit song? `2 points`

 a) "Roni," by Bobby Brown
 b) "B.B.D. (I Thought It Was Me)?" by Bell Biv DeVoe
 c) "If It Isn't Love," by New Edition
 d) "Sensitivity," by Ralph Tresvant

79. Which song includes these lyrics: "You light my fire/I feel alive with you, baby"? `2 points`

 a) the Isley Brothers' "Summer Breeze"
 b) the Gap Band's "Outstanding"
 c) Rick James and Teena Marie's "Fire and Desire"
 d) Rufus and Chaka Khan's "Sweet Thing"

80. Which song intones, "Tell your sons and daughters what the struggle brings"? `2 points`

 a) "Let's Go Crazy"
 b) "Black Butterfly"
 c) "Let's Hear It For the Boy"
 d) "So Fine"

[Answers on page 130]

What's Your HI-FI Q?

SCOTT'S #**7** PICK FOR BEST ALBUMS OF THE 1980s:

Hotter Than July,
Stevie Wonder (1980)

Stevie stepped into the new decade with a muscular, melodious affair that literally changed the world. Not only did he provide Michael Jackson with his finest background per-formance ("All I Do"); not only did he tributize Brother Bob Marley ("Master Blaster"); not only did he provide us with his single finest eighties ballad ("Rocket Love")— Stevie also wrote the black folks' version of "Happy Birthday to You." Tell me you haven't been to a b-day party since 1980 where somebody, if not everybody, broke into a joyous shout of Stevie's tribute to Martin Luther King, Jr.? And whose birthday is not a national holiday? Enough said.

***Essential tracks:** "As If You'd Read My Mind" and "Lately."*

81. Who wrote the following lyrics: "Baby, baby when I look at you/ I get a warm feeling inside"? `2 points`

a) Chaka Khan
b) Prince
c) James Mtume
d) Stevie Wonder

82. Which backup-singer-turned-solo-star sang, "Congratulations/I thought it would have been me"? `2 points`

a) Cheryl Lynn
b) Luther Vandross
c) Vesta Williams
d) Deniece Williams

83. Who uses "Oil of Olay because [his/her] skin gets pale"? `2 points`

a) Notorious B.I.G.
b) Slick Rick
c) Mariah Carey
d) Will Smith

84. Which song begins, "Flower's bloomin', mornin' dew/And the beauty seems to say"? `2 points`

a) "Never Too Much"
b) "Glow of Love"
c) "Shake Your Groove Thing"
d) "Change"

85. Who sang these lyrics in 1984: "Ice cream castles in the summertime"? `2 points`

a) the Time
b) the Commodores
c) the Dazz Band
d) the Main Ingredient

86. Which chanteuse sang these lyrics on her debut album: "My heart's on fire with desire/'Cause I love you"? **2 points**

a) Stacy Lattisaw
b) Janet Jackson
c) Jody Watley
d) Karyn White

87. Who wrote "Your love's so good/Deserves an encore"? **5 points**

a) Jimmy Jam and Terry Lewis
b) L.A. Reid and Babyface
c) Ashford and Simpson
d) Prince

TV & VIDEO

88. In which 1987 music video did Wesley Snipes play the lead gangsta?

a) "Beat It"
b) "Smooth Criminal"
c) "Dirty Diana"
d) "Bad"

89. Who dances through the opening credits of *Do the Right Thing*?

a) Jennifer Lopez
b) Rosie Perez
c) Jody Watley
d) Janet Jackson

90. Which Janet Jackson video utilizes the "one-take" effect?

a) "Escapade"
b) "When I Think of You"
c) "Miss You Much"
d) "Let's Wait Awhile"

[Answers on page 131]

SMOKEY'S #**7** PICK FOR
BEST ALBUMS OF THE 1980s:

**Rhythm Nation 1814,
*Janet Jackson (1989)***

When musicians reach for a higher purpose, you often end up with a bland set of good ideas. But when Jam and Lewis threw a thunderous Sly Stone bass line under Janet's call to arms, the result was stunning. That they were able to smooth it out ("Livin' in a World"), rock it out ("The Knowledge"), and turn Ms. Jackson into a thoroughly sexy love object ("Someday Is Tonight"), all under the same community theme, was even more impressive.

Essential tracks: "Miss You Much" and "Love Would Never Do (Without You)."

L.L. COOL J

91. Bobby Brown's hit "On Our Own" appears on what motion picture soundtrack?

a) *Beverly Hills Cop II*
b) *Rocky IV*
c) *Ghostbusters II*
d) *Look Who's Talking Too*

92. In which video did L.L. Cool J play both cameraman and star?

a) "Around the Way Girl"
b) "Jingling Baby"
c) "Doin It"
d) "Phenomenon"

93. Which song is subtitled the "Love Theme for *General Hospital*"?

a) "Endless Love"
b) "Baby, Come to Me"
c) "How Do You Keep the Music Playing"
d) "I Just Can't Stop Loving You"

94. Which Prince video comprises a black screen with lyrics scrolling across the bottom? 5 points

a) "Sign 'O' the Times"
b) "When 2 R in Love"
c) "Alphabet St."
d) "I Hate U"

SCOTT'S #**6** PICK FOR BEST ALBUMS OF THE 1980s:

It Takes a Nation of Millions to Hold Us Back, *Public Enemy (1988)*

This album is an uncompromising statement of blackness that put the world on notice to the plight of America's inner cities. At no other time has hip-hop had as much power to mobilize as when Chuck D brought the noise.

Essential tracks: *"Don't Believe the Hype" and "Night of the Living Baseheads."*

[Answers on page 131]

ALL TOGETHER NOW (GROUPS)

95. Which Jamaican-born actress/musician has co-starred with both Eddie Murphy and Arnold Schwarzenegger?

a) Rita Marley
b) Foxy Brown
c) Lauryn Hill
d) Grace Jones

96. In 1988, which rap duo claimed "we're gifted and we're going far"?

a) Brand Nubian
b) Salt-n-Pepa
c) Audio Two
d) Run-DMC

97. Ray Parker, Jr., sang with which group before his solo success?

a) Ray of Light
b) Raydio
c) Ray J
d) Rays of Love

98. What does EPMD stand for?

a) Erick and Parrish Makin' Dollars
b) Every Playa Makes Ducats
c) Enuf Pimps Makin' Dough
d) nothing at all

99. Jam Master Jay is to Run-DMC as Cut Creator is to:

a) Snoop Doggy Dogg
b) L.L. Cool J
c) Notorious B.I.G.
d) Mobb Deep

SMOKEY'S **#6** PICK FOR
BEST ALBUMS OF THE 1980s:

It Takes a Nation of Millions to Hold Us Back, *Public Enemy* (1988)

A political manifesto of the highest order, Chuck D asked the people—black people—to "don't believe the hype" and simply "bring the noise!" The result of Chuck D's purposeful, college-educated lyrics and the Bomb Squad's screeching soundscapes, hip-hop's power has never been so well actualized. Imagine our progress if this was always the sound of the inner city.

Essential tracks: "Night of the Living Baseheads" and "Black Steel in the Hour of Chaos."

[Answers on page 131]

DE LA SOUL

100. Before her "Sweetest Taboo" single in 1986, Sade hit with what song?

a) "No Ordinary Love"
b) "Cherish the Day"
c) "King of Sorrow"
d) "Smooth Operator"

101. The Mary Jane Girls originally sang backup for which funk artist?

a) Prince
b) Rick James
c) Al Green
d) Cameo

102. De La Soul's "Me Myself and I" sampled which funk classic? `2 points`

a) "Dazz," by Brick
b) "(Not Just) Knee Deep," by Funkadelic
c) "Love Hangover," by Diana Ross
d) "Funkin' for Jamaica," by Tom Browne

103. Which label released Run-DMC's *Raising Hell* album?

a) Def Jam
b) Profile
c) Tommy Boy
d) Cold Chillin'

104. Who is NOT featured on Marley Marl's 1989 classic "The Symphony"?

a) Masta Ace
b) Big Daddy Kane
c) L.L. Cool J
d) Kool G Rap

[Answers on page 131]

What's Your HI-FI Q?

105. Which group was often known to boast about their "Jimbrowskis"?

    a) N.W.A
    b) St. Lunatics
    c) De La Soul
    d) the Jungle Brothers

106. Producer Dr. Dre could be found wearing eyeliner and mascara as a member of which group?

    a) N.W.A
    b) Cameo
    c) World Class Wreckin' Crew
    d) the Fearless Four

107. Levert's 1987 *The Big Throwdown* LP earned the trio a Grammy nomination on the strength of which hit?

    a) "Casanova"
    b) "Baby I'm Ready"
    c) "On the Down Low"
    d) "Oooh, This Love Is So"

108. Kool Moe Dee was formerly the head of which old-school hip-hop group?

    a) the Fearless Four
    b) Treacherous Three
    c) Funky Four + 1
    d) Soulsonic Force

109. Cameo lead singer Larry Blackmon attended which famed New York City music academy? `2 points`

    a) Fiorello La Guardia High School of Performing Arts
    b) Fame Conservatory
    c) Juilliard School of Music
    d) School of Hard Knocks

SCOTT'S #**6** PICK FOR BEST SINGLES OF THE 1980s:

"Stay Gold," Stevie Wonder (1983)

For the soundtrack to The Outsiders, *Stevie got S.E. Hinton and put her themes on wax with an eloquence only Stevie knows.*

110. In 1988, before his more famous turn as Dr. Octagon, rapper Kool Keith recorded "Give the Drummer Some" with which Bronx collective? 2 points
    a) Boogie Down Productions
    b) Mobb Deep
    c) Ultramagnetic MCs
    d) the Zulu Nation

111. Who was supposed to be the original lead singer of the Time? 5 points
    a) Babyface
    b) Alexander O'Neal
    c) Jerome Benton
    d) Luther Vandross

112. The late DJ Scott LaRock appeared on only one Boogie Down Productions album. Which was it? 2 points
    a) *Fear of a Black Planet*
    b) *By All Means Necessary*
    c) *Criminal Minded*
    d) *Sex and Violence*

113. The D.O.C.'s 1989 debut album *No One Can Do It Better* featured which hit single? 2 points
    a) "It's Funky Enough"
    b) "Nuthin' But a 'G' Thang"
    c) "Dre Day"
    d) "Gin & Juice"

114. Anita Baker was originally a member of which group? 2 points
    a) After 7
    b) Chapter 8
    c) FourPlay
    d) Vanity 6

SMOKEY'S #6 PICK FOR BEST SINGLES OF THE 1980s:

"I Want to Thank You," Alicia Myers (1982)

Forget Kirk Franklin, Alicia Myers's prayer rocked the masses like no gospel-influenced track ever has. A personal note of thanks to the Lord for sending her "someone that loves me." This club favorite proved that no matter your creed or religious beliefs, a grand groove is always the great equalizer. "Thank you, Father!"

[Answers on page 131]

AFRIKA BAMBAATAA

115. Regina Belle sang with which group before starting her solo career? `2 points`

a) the O'Jays
b) the Manhattans
c) the Commodores
d) New Edition

116. Afrika Bambaataa's Soulsonic Force was made up of which three MCs? `2 points`

a) Melle Mell, G.L.O.B.E., Whiz Kid
b) G.L.O.B.E., Pow Wow, Mr. Biggs
c) Flavor Flav, Terminator X, Chuck D
d) Kool Moe Dee, Whiz Kid, Pow Wow

TWO THE HARD WAY (DUETS)

117. With whom did Run-DMC duet on "Walk This Way"?

a) the Rolling Stones
b) Foreigner
c) Aerosmith
d) Judas Priest

118. Scottish-born singer Sheena Easton was nominated for a Grammy Award for which duet with his royal badness?

a) "I Just Can't Stop Lovin' You"
b) "U Got the Look"
c) "Super Freak"
d) "Faith"

[Answers on page 131]

What's Your HI-FI Q?

119. With whom did Cherrelle sing the lyrics "Sunday, Monday, Tuesday, Wednesday, Thursday, Friday, Saturday love"?

a) Keith Sweat
b) Lillo Thomas
c) Alexander O'Neal
d) Jeffrey Osbourne

BONUS INTERNET QUESTION: Can you name the duets they've recorded together?

120. On which Whitney Houston album did she duet with her mother, Cissy?

a) *I'm Your Baby Tonight*
b) *Whitney*
c) *My Love Is Your Love*
d) *Whitney Houston*

121. Who duetted with Queen Latifah on the 1989 track "Ladies First"?

a) Foxy Brown
b) Lil' Kim
c) Roxanne Shanté
d) Monie Love

122. Which female singer has Michael Jackson NOT duetted with?

a) Siedah Garrett
b) Janet Jackson
c) Patti Austin
d) Mary J. Blige

SCOTT'S #**5** PICK FOR BEST SINGLES OF THE 1980s:

"Sexual Healing," Marvin Gaye (1982)

Did he somehow know that this would be his last real statement? Probably not ... But, oh, what a last word!

123. Babyface did backup on whose hit, "Love Makes Things Happen"?
a) Karyn White
b) Cherrelle
c) Pebbles
d) Jody Watley

124. Siedah Garrett teamed with which ex-Temptations singer for "Don't Look Any Further"? `2 points`
a) Eddie Kendricks
b) Dennis Edwards
c) David Ruffin
d) Glen Leonard

125. Who duetted with Aretha Franklin on "I Knew You Were Waiting for Me"? `2 points`
a) Boy George
b) George Michael
c) Robert Palmer
d) Mick Jones

126. Who duetted with Aretha Franklin on "Sisters Are Doing It for Themselves"? `2 points`
a) Cyndi Lauper
b) Annie Lennox
c) Boy George
d) Taylor Dayne

SMOKEY'S #**5** PICK FOR
BEST SINGLES OF THE 1980s:

"Anna Stesia," Prince (1988)

While the album was shrouded in the controversy surrounding Prince's naked body on the album cover, Lovesexy was the most beautiful book of verse the Minneapolis genius ever created. This guitar-drenched call to arms finally saw Prince find deliverance from his loneliness and motivated arenas full of people to chant "Love Is God, God Is Love" throughout his 1988 national tour.

What's Your HI-FI Q?

SCOTT'S #5 PICK FOR BEST ALBUMS OF THE 1980s:

3 Feet High and Rising, *De La Soul* (1989)

We always talk about things going to the "next level." This debut was next level before "next level" became what we called things like this. Other than maybe The Bomb Squad's sonic nuke attack with Public Enemy, this album did more to create a sound than anything else in post–Run-DMC hip-hop. Prince Paul's production gave De La a playground of such loopy grandeur that their rhymes took on a mythic presence in a rap world rife with struggle and pain.

Essential tracks: the entire album.

127. How many times did Michael Jackson duet with Paul McCartney? `2 points`

   a) once
   b) twice
   c) thrice
   d) never

BONUS INTERNET QUESTION: Can you name the songs?

128. A former bandmate of jazz legend Miles Davis and bassist Ron Carter composed which 1983 crossover hip-hop hit? `2 points`

   a) "Rock It"
   b) "Pack Jam"
   c) "The Show"
   d) "Zulu Groove"

129. Which of the following Jackson brothers duetted with Whitney Houston? `2 points`

   a) Jermaine
   b) Michael
   c) Tito
   d) Randy

130. With which soul diva has Stevie Wonder NEVER duetted? `5 points`

   a) Dionne Warwick
   b) Syreeta Wright
   c) Aretha Franklin
   d) Donna Summer

THE KNOB-TWIRLERS
(WRITERS AND PRODUCERS)

131. LaFace Records was founded in 1989 by which former recording duo?

a) L.A. Reid and Kenneth Edmonds
b) Latonya Blige and Babyface
c) L.L. Cool J and Scarface
d) Jimmy Jam and Terry Lewis

BONUS INTERNET QUESTION: Who was the first artist released on LaFace Records?

132. Which song did Prince NOT write? 2 points

a) TLC's "Waterfalls"
b) the Bangles' "Manic Monday"
c) Sheena Easton's "Sugar Walls"
d) TLC's "Give It Up"

133. Who wrote and produced Eddie Murphy's first Top 40 hit, "Party All the Time"? 2 points

a) Stevie Wonder
b) Rick James
c) George Clinton
d) Quincy Jones

134. Gerald Brown, Delisa Davis, Micki Free, and Sidney Justin were all, at some point, members of which R&B group?

a) Atlantic Starr
b) Shalamar
c) the S.O.S. Band
d) the Soul City Orchestra

SMOKEY'S #5 PICK FOR
BEST ALBUMS OF THE 1980s:

Club Classics, Vol. 1,
Soul II Soul (1989)

The best soul music effortlessly moves your body, engaging the listener in spontaneous acts of joyful head-nodding. When Jazzie B., producer Nellee Hooper, and vocalist Caron Wheeler dropped their British drum-and-bass signature on American airwaves, no one could stop grooving. It was beautiful music, thoughtful, inspirational, and instantly memorable.

Essential tracks: "Back to Life" and "Keep On Moving."

[Answers on page 131]

LISA LISA

135. Which Prince-composed song was NOT recorded by Chaka Khan? `2 points`

a) "Eternity"
b) "Ain't Nobody"
c) "777-9311"
d) "I Feel for You"

136. "Driving down those city streets/Waiting to get to down . . ." are the opening lyrics to a hit by which disco diva?

a) Gloria Gaynor
b) Donna Summer
c) Diana Ross
d) Grace Jones

137. Stevie Wonder produced which reggae-based hit?

a) Musical Youth's "Pass the Dutchie"
b) Third World's "Try Jah Love"
c) Grace Jones's "Pull Up to the Bumper"
d) Lionel Richie's "All Night Long"

138. Almost a decade before collaborating with the Backstreet Boys, which production outfit worked with singer Lisa Lisa?

a) Full Force
b) Cult Jam
c) Force MDs
d) Jimmy Jam and Terry Lewis

139. After musicians Jimmy Jam and Terry Lewis were fired from the Time, who did the Minneapolis duo move on to produce? `2 points`

a) the Revolution
b) Janet Jackson
c) the S.O.S. Band
d) Gerald Levert

[Answers on page 131]

SCOTT'S **#4** PICK FOR BEST ALBUMS OF THE 1980s:

Street Songs, *Rick James (1980)*

For a minute there, in the satyr-genius battle between Rick James and Prince, Rick was leading in the polls, flinging off effortless dance cuts and slick ballads that updated the Motown sound without losing the dedication to strong songwriting and virtuoso musicianship. Street Songs was sizzling street music with an orchestrated flair—ballads to make your mama cry ("Fire and Desire") and dance cuts that made pop radio go "oh" ("Superfreak"). We know how this movie ended, but while it was being told there wasn't a much better soundtrack.

Essential track: "Give It to Me, Baby."

ANITA BAKER

140. Who wrote and produced Diana Ross's "Swept Away"? `2 points`

a) Michael Jackson
b) Daryl Hall
c) John Oates
d) Jermaine Jackson

141. Who wrote and produced Diana Ross's "Muscles"? `2 points`

a) Lionel Richie
b) Mick Jagger
c) Michael Jackson
d) Barry Gibb

142. Who wrote and produced Dionne Warwick's "Heartbreaker"? `2 points`

a) Barry Gibb
b) David Bowie
c) George Michael
d) Paul Young

143. Which former child star produced Janet Jackson's first album?
`2 points`

a) Michael Jackson
b) Leon Sylvers
c) Donny Osmond
d) Teddy Riley

GUEST STARS

144. Which sister group sang backup on Anita Baker's *Giving You the Best That I Got* album? `5 points`

a) Sister Sledge
b) the Clark Sisters
c) the Emotions
d) Perri

[Answers on page 131]

SMOKEY'S #**4** PICK FOR
BEST ALBUMS OF THE 1980s:

**3 Feet High and Rising,
De La Soul (1989)**

A hip-hop album that begins with a Monkees-inspired uptempo comedy track like "The Magic Number" had to have been created miles away from the land of ghetto realness. But even the most hard-rock MC couldn't resist the good feelings these Long Island kids so openly relished. With thanks due to producer Prince Paul, the album's true triumph was that it showed us just how much the hip-hop language is capable of.

Essential tracks: "Jenifa Taught Me (Derwin's Revenge)," "Potholes In My Lawn," and "Buddy."

What's Your HI-FI Q?

145. Who provided a memorable backing vocal on Steve Winwood's "Higher Love"?

a) Patti LaBelle
b) Gwen Guthrie
c) Chaka Khan
d) Vesta Williams

146. With whom did Luther Vandross record "If This World Were Mine" in 1982?

a) Diana Ross
b) Cheryl Lynn
c) Teena Marie
d) Lisa Fischer

SCOTT'S #**4** PICK FOR
BEST SINGLES OF THE
1980s:

"Do You Love What You Feel"
Rufus featuring Chaka Khan
(1980)

Disco as disco should be: Quincy gave the group a polish and sheen they hadn't had before. This was Chaka's return after doing the solo thing, and she sounds right at home, dodging in and out of the ad-libs alongside Tony Maiden.

147. Who was the first person ever to lay a rap down for Michael Jackson? `2 points`

a) Treach
b) Vincent Price
c) Notorious B.I.G.
d) Heavy D

148. Which actress can be heard whispering on Prince's "Scandalous" maxi-single? `5 points`

a) Sharon Stone
b) Apollonia
c) Kim Basinger
d) Cindy Crawford

149. Which eighties R&B group reunited to sing backup for Babyface's cover of their hit, "This Is for the Lover in You"?

a) Klymaxx
b) the Mary Jane Girls
c) Shalamar
d) the Cover Girls

MORE GENERAL INTEREST

Okay, you've gotten this far, so we're giving you more general questions to test your mettle. Only thing is, we're talking four-star general with a few easy calls thrown in for good measure. Things are a little harder this time around—think of this as a fade-out with some great improvs, before the next record comes on.

150. On which Prince album is the name of his band, the Revolution printed backward?

a) *Controversy*
b) *Purple Rain*
c) *1999*
d) *Around the World in a Day*

151. Michael Jackson's *Thriller* is the biggest-selling solo LP of all time, with sales exceeding . . .

a) 10 million
b) 20 million
c) 40 million
d) 100 million

152. Which of the following legends was NOT in *The Blues Brothers?*

a) Cab Calloway
b) Chaka Khan
c) James Brown
d) Aretha Franklin

153. Who sang the theme song for *Mad Max Beyond Thunderdome?*

a) Tina Turner
b) Chaka Khan
c) Angela Bassett
d) Grace Jones

SMOKEY'S **#4** PICK FOR BEST SINGLES OF THE 1980s:

***"The Adventures of Grandmaster Flash on the Wheels of Steel,"* Grandmaster Flash and the Furious Five (1981)**

Never before had a party record blended cutting and scratching so seamlessly. Flash, using beats and vocals from Chic's "Good Times," Blondie's "Rapture," and Queen's "Another One Bites the Dust," created a new composition that still stands as one of the finest representations of the hip-hop aesthetic.

[Answers on page 131]

MICHAEL JACKSON

154. On which 1983 TV special did Michael Jackson debut the moonwalk?

a) MTV Video Music Awards
b) the Grammy Awards
c) Motown 25th Anniversary Special
d) Kennedy Center Honors

155. Before Alanis Morissette broke it in 1995, which artist held the record for the biggest-selling debut album?

a) Madonna
b) Michael Jackson
c) Ricky Martin
d) Whitney Houston

156. Which ballad begins "A chair is still a chair"?

a) "Adore"
b) "Since I Lost My Baby"
c) "A House Is Not a Home"
d) "Here and Now"

157. Which song begins "Kissing like a bandit, stealing time"?

a) "Anniversary," by Tony! Toni! Toné!
b) "Creepin'," by Luther Vandross
c) "Saving All My Love for You," by Whitney Houston
d) "Wishing Well," by Terence Trent D'Arby

158. Which of the following Whitney Houston songs was NOT a remake?

a) "The Greatest Love of All"
b) "It's Not Right, but It's Okay"
c) "I'm Every Woman"
d) "I Will Always Love You"

[Answers on page 131]

SCOTT'S #**3** PICK FOR BEST ALBUMS OF THE 1980s:

Sign 'O' the Times, *Prince (1987)*

Six years after Dirty Mind *confirmed his many gifts, and just three years after* Purple Rain *defined an era, Prince presented the world with his version of* Songs in the Key of Life *meets the Rolling Stones'* Exile on Main Street. *This was his world-weary double album that managed to find some celebration amid the low-slung observations about the state of the world. Manic in its eclectic soundscape, it somehow found a central vibe of salvation. It includes, arguably, his best ballad ("Adore"), his best pop pastiche ("The Ballad of Dorothy Parker"), and his best religious statement ("The Cross"), Sign was a mid-decade revelation.*

Essential track: "I Could Never Take the Place of Your Man."

PUBLIC ENEMY

159. What song begins with "Everybody's talking all this stuff about me"?

a) "My Prerogative," by Bobby Brown
b) "Rub You the Right Way," by Johnny Gill
c) "I Want Her," by Keith Sweat
d) "Rumors," by Club Nouveau

160. Production duos L.A. Reid and Babyface and Jimmy Jam and Terry Lewis worked together to produce whose debut album?

a) Bobby Brown
b) Bell Biv DeVoe
c) Janet Jackson
d) Johnny Gill

161. In 1987, which singer followed up two dance hits with the ballad "Anything for You"?

a) Gloria Estefan
b) Whitney Houston
c) Lisa Fischer
d) Paula Abdul

162. Which of the following hit singles was NOT on L.L. Cool J's 1985 debut LP, *Radio*?

a) "Rock the Bells"
b) "I Need a Beat"
c) "I Need Love"
d) "I Can't Live Without My Radio"

163. Which Public Enemy album came out THIRD?

a) *It Takes a Nation of Millions to Hold Us Back*
b) *Fear of a Black Planet*
c) *Apocalypse '91 . . . The Enemy Strikes Black*
d) *Yo! Bum Rush the Show*

SMOKEY'S **#3** PICK FOR
BEST ALBUMS OF THE 1980s:

Run-DMC, *Run-DMC* (1984)

Hip-hop's first commercial champions, Joseph Simmons and Darryl McDaniels brought Adidas sneakers and Lee jeans to a place B-boys never thought possible— they took it to the bank. Hip-hop would never look back. Just don't forget to thank Rick Rubin and his love for that loud-ass electric guitar.

Essential tracks: "Rock Box" and "Sucker MCs."

[Answers on page 131]

RAKIM

164. Which song opened with the proclamation "Too black, too strong"?

   a) "Proud to Be Black," by Run-DMC
   b) "All for One," by Brand Nubian
   c) "Happy Birthday," by Stevie Wonder
   d) "Bring the Noise," by Public Enemy

165. In 1989, which MC questioned the blackness of radio stations?

   a) L.L. Cool J
   b) Chuck D
   c) KRS-One
   d) Rakim

166. Which of the following was NOT the title of a song on De La Soul's *3 Feet High and Rising*?

   a) "Transmitting Live From Mars"
   b) "Tread Water"
   c) "Plant the Seed"
   d) "The Magic Number"

167. Which MC duo sampled Aretha Franklin's "Think" on its debut single?

   a) Black Sheep
   b) 3rd Bass
   c) X-Clan
   d) Pete Rock and C.L. Smooth

168. On which song did Rakim declare, "I don't bug out or chill, don't be acting ill"?

   a) "Move the Crowd"
   b) "Let the Rhythm Hit 'Em"
   c) "Paid in Full"
   d) "Eric B. Is President"

SCOTT'S #**3** PICK FOR BEST SINGLES OF THE 1980s:

"A House Is Not a Home,"
Luther Vandross (1981)

This is a remake. Think fast: Can you tell us who made this first? Timeless, classic, perfect.

[Answers on pages 131–132]

DJ RED ALERT

169. What was the subtitle to Grandmaster Flash and Melle Mel's 1983 hit "White Lines"?

a) (Come Get It)
b) (Don't Get It)
c) (Don't Do It)
d) (Come With It)

170. In 1984, Whodini asked, "how many of us have . . ." what?

a) rhymes
b) friends
c) beats
d) cash money

171. Which Cherrelle song did Robert Palmer remake in 1986?

a) "Everything I Miss at Home"
b) "I Didn't Mean to Turn You On"
c) "Always"
d) "Saturday Love"

172. Which Motown legend's son recorded the paranoia anthem "Somebody's Watching Me"?

a) Berry Gordy
b) Smokey Robinson
c) Marvin Gaye
d) Lamont Dozier

173. What is DJ Red Alert known to have received his name for?

2 points

a) his alarming DJ style
b) his red Afro
c) his knack for shutting down parties
d) his red turntables

[Answers on page 132]

SMOKEY'S **#3** PICK FOR
BEST SINGLES OF THE 1980s:

"A House Is Not a Home," Luther Vandross (1981)

If the opening piano riff can bring a grown woman to tears, then it's got to be something special. While this legendary crooner has graced us with many classic ballads, this soaring love letter stands alone for, shall I say, its breath control. Luther so embodied the words of this song, I bet you'd never believe it was a remake. Listen to it, and you'll never, ever, want to be alone again.

What's Your HI-FI Q?

174. Who shouted on a 1987 single, "Cat, we need you to rap"?
   a) Bobby Brown
   b) Prince
   c) Gerald Levert
   d) Al B. Sure!

175. Prince is to *Batman* as Marvin Gaye is to:
   a) *Let's Do It Again*
   b) *Sounder*
   c) *Trouble Man*
   d) *Uptown Saturday Night*

176. Which "Baby" song came out first?
   a) "Baby Come to Me," by Regina Belle
   b) "Baby Be Mine," by Michael Jackson
   c) "'Til My Baby Comes Home," by Luther Vandross
   d) "Do Me, Baby," by Prince

177. What stage and movie actor duetted with Luther Vandross on "There's Nothing Better Than Love" in 1986?
   a) Gregory Hines
   b) Denzel Washington
   c) Brian Stokes Mitchell
   d) Wesley Snipes

178. With which pop star did Ray Charles duet with on "Baby Grand" in 1986?
   a) Elton John
   b) Bruce Hornsby
   c) Billy Joel
   d) Christopher Cross

179. Which movie soundtrack featured Deniece Williams's "Let's Hear It for the Boy"?

a) *Flashdance*
b) *Footloose*
c) *Porky's*
d) *Breakin'*

180. Who sang "Razzamatazz" on Quincy Jones's 1980 album *The Dude*?

a) Patti LaBelle
b) Patti Austin
c) Patrice Rushen
d) Randy Crawford

181. Lionel Richie's video for "Dancing on the Ceiling" was inspired by a scene from which Fred Astaire movie musical?

a) *Easter Parade*
b) *Royal Wedding*
c) *Top Hat*
d) *The Band Wagon*

182. Which Grace Jones hit includes Jones intoning, mid-song, "Ladies and gentlemen, heeeeere's Grace!"?

a) "Pull Up to the Bumper"
b) "My Jamaican Guy"
c) "Slave to the Rhythm"
d) "Nipple to the Bottle"

183. According to the Dazz Band, "We both are here to have big fun, so let it"?

a) "flip"
b) "whip"
c) "slip"
d) "dip"

SMOKEY'S #**2** PICK FOR
BEST ALBUMS OF THE 1980s:

Paid in Full, *Eric B. & Rakim* (1987)

The most revered album in hip-hop history, Rakim added a lyrical fluidity and a poet's sense of metaphor to Eric B.'s tight, James Brown–influenced beats. It sparked a revolution among MCs who thought all they had to do was get you to "wave your hands like you just don't care!" So few have ever caught up.

***Essential tracks:** "Eric B. Is President" and "Move the Crowd."*

[Answers on page 132]

BIG DADDY KANE

184. Which Prince-founded group originally recorded "Nothing Compares 2 U"?

a) Vanity 6
b) the Family
c) Apollonia 6
d) Madhouse

185. Which diva was nominated for a Tony Award for singing Duke Ellington songs in the Broadway show *Sophisticated Ladies*?

a) Diana Ross
b) Stephanie Mills
c) Melba Moore
d) Phyllis Hyman

186. Which vocal group sang backup for Stephanie Mills when she re-recorded "Home" from *The Wiz* in 1989?

a) New Edition
b) Take 6
c) Tony! Toni! Toné!
d) After 7

187. Which "Never" song came out first?

a) "Never Knew Love Like This Before," by Stephanie Mills
b) "Never Knew Love Like This," by Alexander O'Neal featuring Cherrelle
c) "Never Too Much," by Luther Vandross
d) "Never as Good as the First Time," by Sade

188. Who duetted with Keith Sweat on 1987's "Make It Last Forever"?

a) Siedah Garrett
b) Jacci McGhee
c) Robin S.
d) Chanté Moore

What's Your HI-FI Q?

189. Which duet team performed the theme song for the eighties sitcom *Family Ties*?

   a) Roberta Flack and Peabo Bryson
   b) Luther Vandross and Cheryl Lynn
   c) Johnny Mathis and Deniece Williams
   d) Teddy Pendergrass and Stephanie Mills

190. Which "Let" song came out first?

   a) "Let It Whip," by the Dazz Band
   b) "Let Me Be Your Angel," by Stacy Lattisaw
   c) "Let the Feeling Flow," by Peabo Bryson
   d) "Let the Music Play," by Shannon

191. Which "Let's" song came out first?

   a) "Let's Groove," by Earth, Wind & Fire
   b) "Let's Pretend We're Married," by Prince
   c) "Let's Wait Awhile," by Janet Jackson
   d) "Let's Go Crazy," by Prince

192. Which "Love" song came out first?

   a) "Love Come Down," by Evelyn "Champagne" King
   b) "Love, Need, and Want You Babe," by Patti LaBelle
   c) "Love T.K.O." by Teddy Pendergrass
   d) "Love Is a House," by Force MDs

SCOTT'S #**2** PICK FOR BEST
SINGLES OF THE 1980s:

"Ain't Nobody," Rufus featuring Chaka Khan (1983)

The essence of this group, pared down to a moment so glorious, you wonder if music knows it can be this beautiful.

193. Singer James Ingram cowrote which song on Michael Jackson's *Thriller*?

a) "Billie Jean"
b) "Beat It"
c) "Human Nature"
d) "P.Y.T. (Pretty Young Thing)"

194. Of *Thriller*'s nine cuts, which two did NOT become Top 10 singles?

a) "Human Nature" and "Wanna Be Startin' Somethin'"
b) "Wanna Be Startin' Somethin'" and "The Girl Is Mine"
c) "The Lady in My Life" and "Baby Be Mine"
d) "Baby Be Mine" and "Thriller"

195. Which rock guitar virtuoso played the solo on *Thriller*'s "Beat It"?

a) Eric Clapton
b) Eddie Van Halen
c) Keith Richards
d) Slash

196. What was the name of the nightclub where Prince played in the movie *Purple Rain*?

a) First Avenue
b) Glam Slam
c) Symbol
d) Twin City

SMOKEY'S **#2** PICK FOR
BEST SINGLES OF THE
1980s:

"I'm Coming Out," Diana Ross (1980)

It's gotta be the drums. Diana's finest declaration of independence wins you over with a funked-up snare roll way before the original diva-girl lets us know how happy she is to be doing her own thing. "I want the world to know," she cried, creating this unforgettable anthem of personal power.

[Answers on page 132]

JUNGLE BROTHERS AND
AFRIKA BAMBAATAA

197. The musically talented Wilson brothers of Tulsa, Oklahoma, had several Number One hits as which funk/R&B group?
   a) the O'Jays
   b) the Gap Band
   c) Cameo
   d) the Time

198. In 1985, Daryl Hall and John Oates teamed up for an Apollo Theatre—recorded live album with two former members of which Motown vocal group?
   a) the Temptations
   b) the Four Tops
   c) the Supremes
   d) the Miracles

199. Who wrote and produced the Temptations' 1982 reunion hit "Standing On the Top"?
   a) Lionel Richie
   b) Rick James
   c) Rockwell
   d) Teena Marie

200. According to the 1983 Ashford and Simpson hit, "she wanna live in a high-rise," where?
   a) "way up on the West Side"
   b) "way up on the East Side"
   c) "near the park with a good view"
   d) "just under the blue sky"

DOUG E. FRESH

THE BEST SINGLE OF THE 1980s ACCORDING TO SCOTT

"That Girl," Stevie Wonder (1982)

Music gets no better than this. Simple and direct, a melody to die for, a groove to croon to, background vocals that soar, a complete thought. Perfection.

Honorable Mention:

"Nothing Can Come Between Us," Sade (1988) • "Controversy," Prince (1981) • "Wanna Be Startin' Somethin'," Michael Jackson (1982) • "Rock Box," Run-DMC (1984) • "Rockin' It," Fearless Four (1982)

THE BEST SINGLE OF THE 1980s ACCORDING TO SMOKEY

"The Show/La-Di-Da-Di," Doug E. Fresh and Slick Rick (1985)

For many, this two-sided classic signified the start of their hip-hop lives. It was drums and beat-boxing, storytelling and shit-talkin', and it was all unforgettable. Capturing the energy of a N.Y.C. block party for the hordes of uninitiated, Doug and Rick's back-and-forth banter was playful and irreverent, and proved that the music, already becoming associated with all things negative, could also put a smile on your face and make you have the night of your life. "Okay, party people in the house/You're about to witness something you've never witnessed before . . ." How true that was.

Honorable Mention:

"How Come U Don't Call Me Anymore," Prince (1985) • "The 900 Number," DJ Mark the 45 King (1988) • "Sexual Healing," Marvin Gaye (1982) • "Wanna Be Startin' Somethin'," Michael Jackson (1982) • "The Bridge Is Over," Boogie Down Productions (1987) • "White Lines," Grandmaster Flash and the Furious Five (1983) • "Ain't No Half-Steppin'," Big Daddy Kane (1988) • "I Got It Made," Special Ed (1989) • "1999," Prince (1983)

PRINCE

THE BEST ALBUM OF THE 1980s
ACCORDING TO SCOTT

Dirty Mind, *Prince (1980)*

His Royal Badness abandoned the rules of radio R&B and crafted the single best album of the decade, blending funk licks, sturdy pop songcraft, rock-and-roll swagger, and a pure post-adolescent dedication to sex. We knew he could groove from the first couple of albums, but did we know he had such a singular point of view? Did we know that he was changing the face of pop music as we knew it? Did we know he was a genius with a gift for making sex seem sacred? We found out.

Essential tracks: "When You Were Mine" and "Sister"

Honorable Mention:

Lovesexy, Prince (1988) • *Purple Rain,* Prince (1984) • *Giving You the Best That I Got,* Anita Baker (1988) • *Regina Belle,* Regina Belle (1987) • *Make It Last Forever,* Keith Sweat (1988) • *Don't Be Cruel,* Bobby Brown (1988) • *Gotta Have House, Vol. 1,* Various Artists (1989) • *The Dude,* Quincy Jones (1980) • *Chaka Khan,* Chaka Khan (1980)

THE BEST ALBUM OF THE 1980s
ACCORDING TO SMOKEY

Sign 'O' the Times, *Prince (1987)*

One of the finest double albums ever recorded in any genre, this artistic document perfectly blended all of Prince's varied styles, wrapping funk, rock, gospel, and blues around a simply remarkable set of songs. You danced, you laughed, you cried . . . you played it all again. Michael couldn't touch this talent. Essential tracks: "Adore," "If I Was Your Girlfriend," and "Housequake."

Honorable Mention:

Criminal Minded, Boogie Down Productions (1987) • *Strictly Business,* EPMD (1988) • *Guy,* Guy (1987) • *Thriller,* Michael Jackson (1982) • *Street Songs,* Rick James (1981) • *King of Rock,* Run-DMC (1985) • *Parade (Music From the Motion Picture* Under the Cherry Moon*),* Prince (1986) • *By All Means Necessary,* Boogie Down Productions (1988) • *Control,* Janet Jackson (1986) • *Introducing the Hardline According to Terence Trent D'Arby,* Terence Trent D'Arby (1987)

What's Your HI-FI Q?

ANSWER KEY FOR THE 1980s QUESTIONS

Give yourself one point for each correct answer, unless otherwise indicated. You can find answers to the Bonus Internet Questions at www.blackbookscentral.com and www.hifiq.com.

THE OPENING
1. a
2. b
3. c
4. c
5. b
6. b
7. c
8. c
9. b
10. b
11. d
12. b
13. c
14. b
15. b
16. c (2 points)
17. c (2 points)
18. a (2 points)
19. b (2 points)
20. b (2 points)
21. c (2 points)
22. d (2 points)
23. a (2 points)
24. c (2 points)
25. b (2 points)
26. c (2 points)
27. d (2 points)

28. d (2 points)
29. d (2 points)
30. b (2 points)
31. a (2 points)
32. c (2 points)
33. b (2 points)
34. b (2 points)
35. b
36. a (2 points)
37. a (2 points)
38. b (5 points)
39. a (5 points)
40. d (5 points)

LYRICALLY SPEAKING
41. a
42. b
43. b
44. a
45. b
46. d
47. c
48. c (2 points)
49. d (2 points)
50. b (2 points)
51. b (2 points)
52. b (2 points)
53. c (2 points)

54. a (5 points)
55. c (5 points)
56. c (2 points)
57. c (2 points)
58. a (2 points)
59. a (2 points)
60. b (2 points)
61. b (2 points)
62. b (2 points)
63. c (5 points)
64. b (5 points)
65. b (2 points)
66. b (2 points)
67. d (2 points)
68. c (2 points)
69. c (2 points)
70. d (2 points)
71. d
72. c
73. d
74. c
75. b (2 points)
76. a (2 points)
77. c (2 points)
78. c (2 points)
79. b (2 points)
80. b (2 points)
81. b (2 points)

82. c (2 points)
83. b (2 points)
84. b (2 points)
85. a (2 points)
86. d (2 points)
87. a (5 points)

TV & VIDEO
88. d
89. b
90. b
91. c
92. a
93. b
94. b (5 points)

ALL TOGETHER NOW (GROUPS)
95. d
96. c
97. b
98. a
99. b
100. d
101. b
102. b (2 points)
103. b
104. c
105. d
106. c
107. a
108. b
109. c (2 points)
110. c (2 points)

111. b (5 points)
112. c (2 points)
113. a (2 points)
114. b (2 points)
115. b (2 points)
116. b (2 points)

TWO THE HARD WAY (DUETS)
117. c
118. b
119. c
120. b
121. d
122. d
123. c
124. b (2 points)
125. b (2 points)
126. b (2 points)
127. c (2 points)
128. a (2 points)
129. a (2 points)
130. d (5 points)

THE KNOB-TWIRLERS (WRITERS AND PRODUCERS)
131. a
132. a (2 points)
133. b (2 points)
134. b
135. c (2 points)
136. d
137. b
138. a

139. c (2 points)
140. b (2 points)
141. c (2 points)
142. a (2 points)
143. b (2 points)

GUEST STARS
144. d (5 points)
145. c
146. b
147. b (2 points)
148. c (5 points)
149. c

MORE GENERAL INTEREST
150. c
151. c
152. c
153. c
154. a
155. d
156. c
157. d
158. b
159. a
160. d
161. a
162. c
163. b
164. d
165. b
166. c
167. b

Answers

What's Your HI-FI Q?

168. d
169. c
170. b
171. b
172. a
173. b (2 points)
174. b
175. c
176. d
177. a
178. c
179. b
180. b

181. b
182. c
183. b
184. b
185. d
186. b
187. a
188. b
189. c
190. b
191. a
192. c
193. d

194. c
195. b
196. a
197. b
198. a
199. b
200. b

TOTAL POSSIBLE SCORE: 328 points

ENTER YOUR SCORE HERE ☐

Press Pause

THE FIVE BEST DEBUT SINGLES

1. "The Rain (Supa Dupa Fly)" Missy Elliott (1997)

A breezy harbinger of the fearless creativity we would witness over the next few years from Missy and her beatmaster partner Timbaland, this slow-paced piece of moody blues disguised as a hip-hop cut introduced us to sounds never heard before and laid the blueprint for the kind of melodic scatting that would soon dominate R&B.

2. "O.P.P." Naughty by Nature (1991)

Opening with the two most memorable notes in all of hip-hop (thanks to a Jackson 5 "I Want You Back" sample), this summer jam quickly became rap music's first boy-girl anthem. Who would have thought that Treach would become such an icon of ruffneck aggression after such playful roots? "Arm me with harmony . . ."

3. "Hold On," En Vogue (1990)

Even though producers Denzil Foster and Thomas McElroy cleverly used the same beat L.L. Cool J was rocking clubs with only a month prior, this girl group's luscious harmonies made up for the jack in a big way. Sexy, mature, and armed with the kind of full-bodied soul that was sorely missing from the pop landscape, En Vogue instantly became the quartet to die for.

4. "Brown Sugar," D'Angelo (1995)

While it's historically naive to label a young talent a "genius" after one album, D'Angelo's organ-drenched groove clearly displayed a respect for R&B's masters. The best part of the genre-creating single may in fact be the Marvin-esque whispers that hide behind every verse.

5. "You Used to Love Me," Faith Evans (1995)

Sorrow songs have defined the female half of rhythm and blues ever since Bessie Smith wailed away in a beat-up roadside honky-tonk. Here, the blond diva of the nineties sat in a fat leather armchair and gracefully purred her way into that legacy—without a guest verse from her then husband. "I remember the way you used to love me . . ."

THE FIVE BEST HIP-HOP POSSE RECORDS

1. "Scenario," A Tribe Called Quest featuring Leaders of the New School (1991)

It's amazing what three notes and a great hook can add up to. In this case it's the score for hip-hop's most

memorable group performance. The chemistry between these five different MCs was electric: Phife mused, Dinco scatted, Q-Tip and Charlie Brown charmed us with their musical call and response while Busta Rhymes, the self-proclaimed dungeon dragon, first dropped the beat, then exploded like the true monster he is. "Oh my gosh, oh my gosh!" It has never been done better.

2. "Buddy," De La Soul featuring Jungle Brothers and Q-Tip (1989)

Has anyone figured out what "meeenie, meeenie, meeenie" means anyway? Never mind, because there's probably not a more memorized song in all of hip-hop. De La fans who swear their idols never say anything that isn't profound or uplifting pretend to forget what the subject of this song is. No matter, because this six-minute sexcapade—and De La's most lasting song—will never be forgotten. "Hold up, wait a minute!"

3. "Flava N Ya Ear" (remix), Craig Mack featuring the Notorious B.I.G., Rampage, L.L. Cool J, and Busta Rhymes (1994)

Maybe it was Puff's clicking of the bottles or Biggie's opening line ("Niggas is mad I get more butt than ashtrays") but this ball of fire became an instant classic the moment it made the music-heavy summer of '94 even hotter. Producer Easy Mo Bee also flipped this remix beat into something stronger than the original. Imagine that.

4. "Ain't No Fun," Snoop Doggy Dogg featuring Nate Dogg, Kurupt, and Warren G (1993)

With lyrics as misogynistic as these, it's a miracle C. Delores Tucker didn't ban this song before it was even conceived. To the contrary, this L.A. classic had such an irresistible groove, dance halls full of independent women from coast to coast actually chanted the hook like it was an Aretha anthem. It must have been the liquor.

5. "4, 3, 2, 1," L.L. Cool J featuring Redman, Method Man, Canibus, and DMX (1997)

Overshadowed by the conflict between Canibus and L.L. Cool J that was spawned by this record, the snare and horn jam wouldn't have made such memorable penetration into the hip-hop psyche without such a hot beat. Too bad Mr. "Snatch your crown . . ." couldn't turn this moment into a longer career.

Honorable mention:

"Niggaz Done Started Something," DMX featuring the LOX and Mase (1998)

What's Your HI-FI Q?

THE FIVE BEST SEX JAMS OF THE 90s

If the nineties can be defined by sex and foolishness, than what better list is there to set off the decade? But any list of sex-inducing hip-hop and rhythm and blues must begin with the masters, and all masters (whether they are of the loving, pimping, begging, or just straight horny type) must have a large body of work. And that makes it hard.

So here's to the artists that have made it their business to get between our sheets and set the mood. Alas, not the mood of love but the mood of sex. Pure, unadulterated passion. No names necessary.

1. "Shhh," Prince and the New Power Generation (1995)

No amateurs allowed. Although this warning is perhaps unnecessary, since anyone without serious sex game is not going to survive the intro drumroll. But if you do, mountains of pleasure await. Here, Prince's operatic song-writing is in full gear as is his skill for making our most profane desires a spiritual priority. "I'd rather wait till everyone's fast asleep/And do it on the kitchen on the tabletop . . ." So don't get distracted by the anonymous woman that purrs behind the groove; instead, focus on the man's soaring falsetto and the electric guitar that fights the whole way to be heard until, after another climactic drumroll, it finally gets to release itself all over the last two minutes. Get married to "Adore." Make twins to this.

2. "Bump N' Grind (Old School mix)," R. Kelly (1994)

The "Down Low" remix is R's best piece of sexual storytelling, but the guitar-intro version of "Bump N' Grind" is clearly his best groove. A gorgeous, synthesized rhythm section accompanies this set of not-so-subtle suggestions, allowing the author to ensure that his plea for ass never sounds desperate. Instead, the music wins, swooping up the listener in a wave of trancelike chords. Late-night rescue at its best. "I don't see nothing wrong . . ."

3. "Freek 'n You," Jodeci (1995)

"Every time I close my eyes, I wake up feeling so horny. . . ." This jam starts blunt and ends dramatic—just like most good, testosterone-heavy encounters. Here, the group's sweeping chorus grandly backs up K-Ci's incessant wailing and DeVante's playful synth teasing. But if that isn't enough to get the grind going, check the remix with Raekwon of the Wu.

4. "Anytime, Anyplace," Janet Jackson (1993)

A seven-minute lights-out affair that reminds all participants of Janet's earlier moments like *"Funny How Time Flies"* and *"Someday Is Tonight,"* this jam lets a rhythm guitar and hand claps do all the work—until five minutes in, when the moaning starts. No one has better breath control. *"I don't want to stop just because/People walking by are watching us . . ."* The feeling's mutual.

5. "Nobody," Keith Sweat (1996)

Nobody begs better than this skinny, high-pitched Harlem loverman, but when he gets cocky with the verse, he reaches new heights. The beat is just slow enough to play out each and every line, all the better because this jam is a duet. *"And who can love you like me?/Nobody."* I didn't think so.

Honorable mention:

"Put It in Your Mouth," Akinyele (1996)
"Doin It," L.L. Cool J (1996)
"Pretty Brown Eyes," Mint Condition (1991)
". . . Til the Cops Come Knockin'," Maxwell (1996)
"(Lay Your Head on My) Pillow," Tony! Toni! Toné! (1994)

Press Play

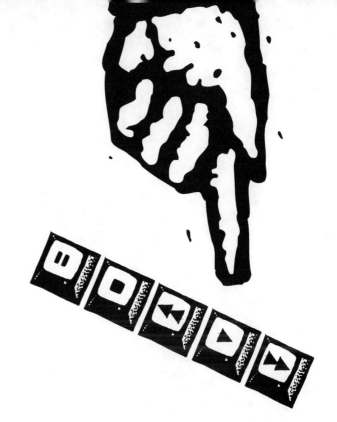

NOTORIOUS B.I.G.

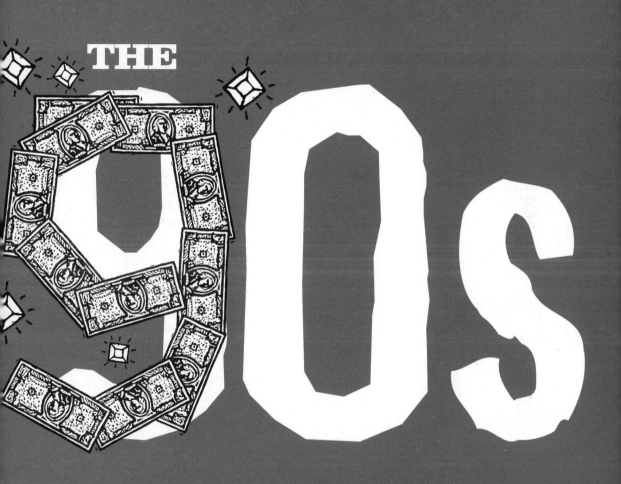

THE 90s

Bling! Bling! Money Changes Everything

What's Your
HI-FI Q?

THE NINETIES: BLING! BLING! MONEY CHANGES EVERYTHING

The Nineties . . . the decade of "bling bling," when De La Soul rhymed about "ring ring" and managed to stay sane when we all seemed to go crazy. In the nineties, we blew up the spot, took everything to the next level, flossed, kicked it, and, most of all, best of all, kept it real. We dissed L.L. Cool J for bling-blinging in the eighties, then decided it was okay to bling-bling in the nineties—once we got all that politics out of our system, once we decided we didn't need any Poor Righteous Teachers or Public Enemies.

Paul Simon once sang that "The words of the prophets are written on the subway walls and tenement halls," and they were, for a minute, in the nineties. The Jungle Brothers and P.E. were educating the nation (the Hip-Hop Nation, as we called it), only now the tenement halls were on a video set and all the world could read the writing on the wall. We were here, we were in gear (in both senses of the word), and everybody had to get used to it.

Producers continued to be kings of the studio, recording singers who could sing their songs and metamorphosing into the moguls who could sign the singers—who would soon be writing their own songs—because publishing was the secret and everybody who was anybody in the industry knew that. And everybody was in the industry: models, actors, singers, stars. Hip-hop's DIY mentality had infiltrated everything under the sun: He got it? Well, yo, then I want it too!

Yeah, it was a wild time in black music. A wild ride, cynical and over-the-top, expensive and expendable—the eighties had finally caught up with black folks. Or had black folks finally caught up with the eighties and flipped it nineties-style? Who knows?

What we do know is that somehow, some way, we lost—Tupac, Biggie, and others—but boy did we gain. Amid all the drama, how did the music get so fresh?

So what do you think about when you think about the nineties?

Answer some of these questions and see if your memories are as strong as Puff Daddy on radio lockdown.

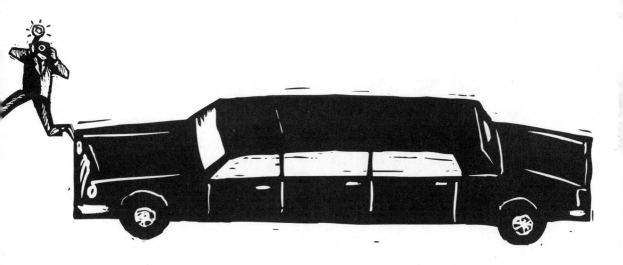

What's Your HI-FI  Q?

THE OPENING

1. In 1991, what author of the R&B hit "I Like" produced Michael Jackson's "Remember the Time"?
   a) Timbaland
   b) Rodney Jerkins
   c) Teddy Riley
   d) Babyface

2. What was the title of Das EFX's debut single that used part of the duo's own name?
   a) "Das Boot"
   b) "They Want Das"
   c) "They Want EFX"
   d) "EFX R US"

3. In 1992, partners Daddy Mack and Mack Daddy released which huge crossover single?
   a) "Jump Around"
   b) "Warm It Up"
   c) "Jump"
   d) "How I Could Just Kill a Man"

4. In 1993, when Tommy Mottola married Mariah Carey, he was president of which record label?
   a) Crave
   b) Sony Music
   c) Def Jam
   d) Columbia Records

SCOTT'S #10 PICK FOR
BEST SINGLES OF THE 1990s:

"And God Created Woman,"
Prince (1992)

Buried on the "symbol" CD, this gem verges on lounge-sounding. But its sleek sexiness and vocal significance border on brilliance.

5. Bay area rapper/label CEO E-40 became a star with which 1993 hit?

a) "Crossroads"
b) "Tennessee"
c) "Fuck tha Police"
d) "Captain Save-a-Hoe"

6. In 1992, Sir Mix-a-Lot sold over 2 million copies of his album *Daddy Mack* on the strength of which single?

a) "Square Dance Rap"
b) "Men in Black"
c) "Rumpshaker"
d) "Baby Got Back"

7. In 1991, who gave us the dance chant "la da dee, la da dah"?

a) CeCe Peniston
b) Deee-Lite
c) Crystal Waters
d) Diana Ross

8. What does "T.A.F.K.A.P." stand for?

a) The Artist Frequently Known to Attack Photographers
b) The Artist Frequently Known to Appear Purple
c) The Artist Formerly Known as Prince
d) The Artist Formerly Known as Symbol

9. Which of the following artists is also a bestselling novelist?

a) Sistah Souljah
b) Mary J. Blige
c) Anita Baker
d) Dawn Robinson

SMOKEY'S #**10** PICK FOR
BEST SINGLES OF THE 1990s:

*"It's All About the Benjamins,"
Puff Daddy & the Family (1997)*

Say what you want about Sean Combs, but these horns and drums are undeniable. The slow, driving beat was thought too hard for the mainstream until the motto of a generation was whispered over the track, and Lil' Kim and a born-again B.I.G. were added to the remix. "Now what y'all wanna do? [You] wanna be ballers, shot callers, brawlers?" Puff was so on fire during this period he filmed three videos for the song, including a rock and a tap-dance version, the latter of which featured a battle with Savion Glover. You had to see it to believe it.

[Answers on page 229]

JAM AND LEWIS

10. Jermaine Dupri is to Xscape as Sean "Puffy" Combs is to:
a) 112
b) Mase
c) Soul for Real
d) Total

11. Which of these acts has NOT been produced by Jimmy Jam and Terry Lewis?
a) Usher
b) Brandy
c) Mary J. Blige
d) Boyz II Men

12. Which R&B classic does En Vogue harmonize at the beginning of "Hold On"?
a) "I'll Be There"
b) "Who's Lovin' You"
c) "Let's Get It On"
d) "Never Can Say Goodbye"

13. Which dancehall star is known as "Mr. Loverman"?
a) Shabba Ranks
b) Cutty Ranks
c) Snow
d) Shaggy

14. Which teen group had a hit called "Candy Rain"?
a) Soul for Real
b) the Boys
c) Another Bad Creation
d) Kris Kross

LIL KIM

15. Who offered the world the idea of *Sex Packets*?

a) Digital Underground
b) De La Soul
c) Digable Planets
d) Damian Dame

16. Washington, D.C.'s, DJ Kool of "Let Me Clear My Throat" fame also started which dance craze?

a) the D.C. Shuffle
b) the Percolator
c) the Humpty Dance
d) the Water Dance

17. Who did Luke teach how to "Knock da Boots"?

a) Jodeci
b) Shai
c) H-Town
d) 'N Sync

18. Which artist "rub-a-dubbed in the back of the club" in Junior M.A.F.I.A.'s "Players Anthem"?

a) Lil' Cease
b) Faith Evans
c) Lil' Kim
d) Yo Yo

19. In 1991, which digitally created duet won a Grammy for Song of the Year?

a) "Unforgettable"
b) "All I Need"
c) "Scream"
d) "Girl U Know It's True"

What's Your HI-FI Q?

SCOTT'S #**10** PICK FOR
BEST ALBUMS OF THE 1990s:

On How Life Is, *Macy Gray* (2000)

When Macy Gray won a Grammy she thanked Chaka Khan, Stevie Wonder, and Prince, among others. I only mention that because I rarely believe other artists when they shout-out the foremothers and fore-fathers who made the music we all "grew up" on. But, I believe that she does listen to—and loves—those geniuses. All you have to do is listen to Macy's record to know that the groove is in her. Her voice may be an acquired taste, but the words that come out of her mouth are some of the truest that radio has heard in years from a new black artist. She makes the list because she truly is carrying on the music movement. She may be a poser at times, but she's never posing about her influences.

***Essential tracks:** "I Try" and "Still."*

20. Produced by DJ Pooh, "At Your Own Risk" helped give which West Coast MC a stellar sophomore LP?
   a) Ice Cube
   b) Snoop Doggy Dogg
   c) King Tee
   d) DJ Quik

21. The title to Atlanta duo OutKast's third album blended which two words together?
   a) Atlanta and Georgia
   b) Andre and Boi
   c) Aquarius and Gemini
   d) funk and Cadillac

22. The 1996 debut album of Crucial Conflict, *The Final Tic,* featured which hit single?
   a) "Rodeo Ride"
   b) "Hay"
   c) "Crossroads"
   d) "Country Grammar"

23. In 1994, former Bad Boy Entertainment star Craig Mack shared promotional campaigns with which artist?
   a) 112
   b) Faith Evans
   c) Shyne
   d) Notorious B.I.G.

24. In 1995, rapper AZ scored a solo hit with the title track to which Wesley Snipes film?
   a) *Jungle Fever*
   b) *Sugar Hill*
   c) *New Jack City*
   d) *Boyz N the Hood*

25. What do performers A+, Chi Ali, and Aaliyah have in common?

a) they were all mentored by hitmaker Barry Hankerson
b) they were all down with the Native Tongues posse
c) they all released debut albums before their 16th birthdays
d) they all won *Star Search* competitions

26. Before they blew up, who was down with ABC and BBD?

a) H-Town
b) Boyz II Men
c) SWV
d) TLC

27. What is a "187"?

a) Smith & Wesson special edition Glock
b) police code for a homicide
c) bus to Riker's Island
d) performance-ready microphone

28. When Chuck D rapped "Motherf**k him and John Wayne," he was referring to whom?

a) Vanilla Ice
b) Ronald Reagan
c) Elvis Presley
d) Michael Bolton

29. To whom is producer Terry Lewis married?

a) Halle Berry
b) Karyn White
c) Anita Baker
d) Alicia Keys

SMOKEY'S **#10** PICK FOR
BEST ALBUMS OF THE 1990s:

Diary of a Mad Band, *Jodeci* **(1993)**

Yearning has always been an essential component of rhythm and blues, and in the early nineties, no one could moan and groan better than K-Ci, JoJo, and the boys. A melody-centered tour de force, the band turned to a darker, grittier, soulful sound to follow the pop poetry of "Stay." They also made it cool for skinny guys to take their shirts off. "Baby I'm beggin'/Baby, I'm beggin', beggin' baby ..."

Essential tracks: "Cry for You" and "What About Us."

METHOD MAN

30. Which entertainer started his career as "Mr. Big Stuff," then went on to become president of Uptown Records?

a) Prince Markie Dee
b) Puff Daddy
c) Heavy D
d) Andre Harrell

31. Which of the following is NOT a Method Man alias?

a) Ticalion Stallion
b) Red-Eyed Bandit
c) Johnny Blaze
d) Ghostface Killah

32. Brian McKnight sang vocals on "I'll Take Her" for which duo's second 1994 hit?

a) Rob Base & D.J. E-Z Rock
b) Ill All Scratch
c) Pete Rock and C.L. Smooth
d) Salt-n-Pepa

33. Which of the following artists CANNOT claim Prince as a one-time producer?

a) Monie Love
b) D'Angelo
c) Sheila E.
d) the Time

34. Kool G Rap teamed up with which DJ for classics like "Ill Street Blues" and "Streets of New York"?

a) Red Alert
b) Kid Capri
c) Polo
d) Eric B.

[Answers on page 229]

35. Which artist's 1991 lawsuit with Gilbert O'Sullivan unwittingly led to the era of "sample clearance"?

a) Chuck D
b) Run-DMC
c) Biz Markie
d) the Beastie Boys

36. Which opera diva performed on Janet Jackson's *Janet*?

a) Jessye Norman
b) Denice Graves
c) Kathleen Battle
d) Leontyne Price

37. Which of the following is NOT the title of an EPMD album?

a) *Business Is Business*
b) *Business Never Personal*
c) *Back to Business*
d) *Unfinished Business*

38. After riding in "Jeeps, Lex Coups, Bimaz & Benz," the Lost Boyz released what ode to a lost girlfriend?

a) "I Used to Love H.E.R."
b) "Brenda's Got a Baby"
c) "What Bitches Want"
d) "Renee"

39. "Scenario," the hip-hop posse cut featuring Busta Rhymes, rapper Charlie Brown, and others, appears on which 1991 album?

a) *A Future Without a Past*
b) *Straight Out the Jungle*
c) *Beats, Rhymes and Life*
d) *The Low End Theory*

SCOTT'S #**9** PICK FOR BEST
SINGLES OF THE 1990s:

"Mind Playing Tricks on Me,"
the Geto Boys (1991)

In which the Geto Boys explain the 'hood life with pinpoint detail. Everything's supposedly bigger in Texas, but these brothers found musical magic in the small stuff.

40. In Common's "I Used To Love H.E.R.," what does "H.E.R." refer to?

a) his microphone
b) Erykah Badu
c) hip-hop culture
d) Lauryn Hill

41. Which rock icon joined Puff Daddy for a live performance at the 1998 MTV Music Awards?

a) David Bowie
b) Sting
c) Lenny Kravitz
d) Eric Clapton

42. Brooklyn duo Cocoa Brovaz recorded the classic 1995 "Bucktown" single under which moniker?

a) Black Moon
b) A Tribe Called Quest
c) the Jungle Brothers
d) Smif-N-Wessun

43. Which two members of Bone Thugs-N-Harmony are siblings?

a) Flesh and Krayzie Bone
b) Flesh and Layzie Bone
c) Eazy-E and the D.O.C.
d) Layzie Bone and Shinehead

44. In 1992, which artist or group made headlines with a brash rap titled "Bush Killa"?

a) Ice-T
b) Paris
c) Public Enemy
d) X-Clan

[Answers on page 229]

SMOKEY'S **#9** PICK FOR
BEST SINGLES OF THE 1990s:

"Ice Cream," Raekwon featuring Ghostface Killah, Method Man, and Cappadonna (1995)

Not to be underestimated as a stereotypical male-only, girl-chasing rave (which it is), this ghetto composition features one of producer RZA's finest soundscapes. Everything is here: the wails and eerie piano, the chopped-up samples and live drum sound. Hip-hop's most creative crew battles styles and everybody wins. Who but the Wu could turn the phrase "the ice cream man is coming" into a call of the wild?

TEDDY RILEY

45. Which artist was NEVER produced by hitmaker Teddy Riley?

a) R. Kelly
b) Kool Moe Dee
c) Aaron Hall
d) Michael Jackson

46. What was on the B side of Wu-Tang Clan's 1993 debut single "Protect Ya Neck"?

a) "C.R.E.A.M."
b) "All I Need"
c) "Method Man"
d) "Bring the Pain"

47. What was the name of Marky Mark's backup group?

a) the White Boys
b) the Funky Bunch
c) the Soul Brothas
d) D12

48. In 1993, Run-DMC DJ Jam Master Jay produced which bangin' club hit? `2 points`

a) "Mo Money Mo Problems"
b) "Jump Around"
c) "Slam"
d) "Toss It Up"

49. For which artist has Puff Daddy NOT done a remix? `2 points`

a) the Police
b) the Jackson 5
c) Michael Jackson
d) KRS-One

SEAN COMBS

50. Which of the following professional athletes is NOT married to a recording artist? `2 points`

a) Mark Jackson of the N.Y. Knicks
b) Gary Sheffield of the Atlanta Braves
c) Derek Jeter of the N.Y. Yankees
d) Rick Fox of the L.A. Lakers

51. The recording label of which producing partnership released records by gospel group Sounds of Blackness? `2 points`

a) Jimmy Jam and Terry Lewis
b) L.A. Reid and Babyface
c) Denzil Foster and Thomas McElroy
d) Reggie Lucas and James Mtume

52. Which of these artists or groups has NOT been produced by Dallas Austin? `2 points`

a) Blue Cantrell
b) TLC
c) Monica
d) Whitney Houston

53. What is Sean "Puffy" Combs nickname a reference to? `5 points`

a) his large head
b) his childhood habit for inflating his chest
c) his preference for large down jackets
d) his smoking habits

54. Which soundtrack album featured the debut of Toni Braxton? `2 points`

a) *The Bodyguard*
b) *Waiting to Exhale*
c) *Boomerang*
d) *Coming to America*

[Answers on page 229]

NAUGHTY BY NATURE

55. Which singer "discovered" TLC? `2 points`

a) Whitney Houston
b) Pebbles
c) Cherrelle
d) T-Boz

56. What was the title of Warren G's debut? `2 points`

a) "Aggravate"
b) "Regulate"
c) "Postulate"
d) "Abbreviate"

57. For the soundtrack to *The Best Man*, four R&B artists recorded "The Best Man I Can Be." Along with R.L., Ginuwine, and Case, who was the fourth singer? `2 points`

a) Johnny Gill
b) Tyrese
c) Maxwell
d) D'Angelo

58. What was Naughty by Nature's 1991 hit "Everything's Gonna Be Alright" originally titled? `2 points`

a) "Problem Child"
b) "Hip-Hop Hooray"
c) "Ghetto Bastard"
d) "It's On"

59. Producer/rapper Khadafi of Capone-N-Noreaga fame has two former aliases. What are they? `2 points`

a) DMX and Earl Simmons
b) Brother J and Jack the Ripper
c) Tragedy and Intelligent Hoodlum
d) Ed Lover and Special Ed

[Answers on page 229]

What's Your HI-FI Q?

SCOTT'S #**9** PICK FOR BEST ALBUMS OF THE 1990s:

Of the Heart, of the Soul, and of the Cross: The Utopian Experience, *P.M. Dawn (1990)*

This album got me into tons of trouble when it first came out. I named it the best debut hip-hop record of the year in Spin *magazine. And I got letters. I was even threatened with having my "ghetto pass" revoked. Okay, I agree: Brand Nubian and Naughty's albums were probably better; they had more street-cred anyway. But, still, when I play this record, I remember the way my ears felt when that "True" sample introduced "Set Adrift on Memory Bliss"—I was simply in heaven. I love this album. No more apologies.*

Essential tracks: "Paper Doll" and "Reality Used to Be a Friend of Mine."

60. **Sean "Puffy" Combs remixed which Grammy-winning Ashford and Simpson duet?** `2 points`
    a) "I'm Coming Out"
    b) "You're All I Need"
    c) "Every Breath You Take"
    d) "I'm Every Woman"

61. **What was the full stage name of 2 Live Crew's Luke?** `2 points`
    a) Luther Campbell
    b) Luke Perry
    c) Luther Vandross
    d) Luke Skyywalker

62. **What was Prince's first recording using a symbol as a moniker?** `2 points`
    a) "When Doves Cry"
    b) "I Hate U"
    c) "The Most Beautiful Girl in the World"
    d) *Girl 6* soundtrack

63. **What was Notorious B.I.G.'s first single?** `2 points`
    a) "Juicy"
    b) "Mo Money Mo Problems"
    c) "Party and Bullshit"
    d) "One More Chance"

64. Which of the following artists has NOT become an ordained minister? 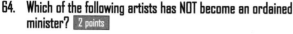 2 points

a) DJ Run
b) James Brown
c) Al Green
d) Mase

65. What do the initials used by one-half of the rapping duo Showbiz & A.G. stand for? 5 points

a) Adam Grant
b) a gangsta
c) Andre the Giant
d) After God

66. What was the first remix Sean "Puffy" Combs ever produced? 2 points

a) "Love No Limit," by Mary J. Blige
b) "Juicy," by Notorious B.I.G.
c) "Come and Talk to Me," by Jodeci
d) "All I Need," by Method Man featuring Mary J. Blige

BONUS INTERNET QUESTION: Which song did he sample from?

67. Miggady-Mark of Wreckx-N-Effect is the brother of which noted music producer? 2 points

a) Dallas Austin
b) Teddy Riley
c) Jermaine Dupri
d) Timbaland

SMOKEY'S #**9** PICK FOR
BEST ALBUMS OF THE 1990s:

Death Certificate, *Ice Cube (1991)*

While Ice Cube's viciously homophobic and misogynistic lyrics demand apologies, the disenfranchisement that fuels his negative passions needs to be explored. And there is no better document for it. As on his debut, AmeriKKKa's Most Wanted, Cube goes ballistic on everything and everyone he sees in the 'hood around him, but this time chooses to add a more club-friendly set of beats to his raving observations.

Essential tracks: "Wrong Nigga to Fuck Wit" and "Black Korea."

PETE ROCK AND C.L. SMOOTH

68. In which song does Prince reveal he's a *Forrest Gump* fan? `2 points`

a) "Dirty Mind"
b) "My Name Is Prince"
c) "I Hate U" (remix)
d) "Diamonds and Pearls"

69. Funkster Neneh Cherry bears what family relationship to jazz trumpeter Don Cherry? `2 points`

a) stepdaughter
b) wife
c) mother
d) none

70. A hologram was used in the 1991 cover packaging of which hit Prince album? `2 points`

a) *The Gold Experience*
b) *Diamonds and Pearls*
c) *Emancipation*
d) *1999*

71. "It's Not a Game" was the club-ready B side to which Pete Rock and C.L. Smooth hit? `2 points`

a) "They Reminisce Over You (T.R.O.Y.)"
b) "Creator"
c) "Lots of Lovin'"
d) "Check the Rhime"

72. What does MAAD stand for in WC and the MAAD Circle? `2 points`

a) Minority Alliance Against Discrimination
b) Mister Attitude Alters Disguise
c) Minority Agitators Against Disses
d) MCs Alliance Against Discrimination

[Answers on page 229]

SCOTT'S #**8** PICK FOR BEST SINGLES OF THE 1990s:

"Tabloid Junkie," Michael Jackson (1995)

The one brilliant thing to come out of the HIStory sessions—urgent and carefree. Jam and Lewis again putting a Jackson among some of the finest sounds available. Listen to MJ's backgrounds. Beautiful.

73. **Which Michigan city gave birth to Ready for the World?**
    `2 points`

    a) Detroit
    b) Ann Arbor
    c) Lansing
    d) Flint

74. **Who is Anthony Terrell Smith better known as?** `2 points`

    a) Young MC
    b) Tone-Lōc
    c) Treach
    d) Busta Rhymes

75. **Long after his hits "The Show" and "Keep Risin' to the Top," Doug E. Fresh could be found touring with?** `2 points`

    a) Prince
    b) the Fugees
    c) Jay-Z
    d) Public Enemy

76. **Yonkers-bred DMX started his hip-hop career as what?**
    `5 points`

    a) a DJ
    b) a beat-box artist
    c) a break dancer
    d) a graffiti artist

77. **Redman's "Sooperman Luva" series was musically inspired by which great soul man?** `2 points`

    a) Marvin Gaye
    b) Al Green
    c) Teddy Pendergrass
    d) Johnny "Guitar" Watson

SMOKEY'S #**8** PICK FOR
BEST SINGLES OF THE 1990s:

"Creep," TLC (1994)

Dallas Austin's best work. This horn-heavy, mid-tempo pop hit anchored Crazysexycool, the Atlanta girl band's sophomore album, and moved the trio away from the bubblegum persona of their earlier material. Here, the harmonies worked, the bass line was hard enough to compete in a hip-hop world, and for a moment, R&B didn't need a guest rapper.

[Answers on page 229]

What's Your HI-FI Q?

78. What producer NEVER laid a track down for the late Notorious B.I.G.? `5 points`
    a) Timbaland
    b) DJ Premier
    c) Mannie Fresh
    d) RZA

79. Who was the last MC to rhyme on Craig Mack's 1994 "Flava in Ya Ear" remix? `5 points`
    a) L.L. Cool J
    b) DMX
    c) Busta Rhymes
    d) Notorious B.I.G.

80. Before *Moesha*, singer/actress Brandy co-starred on which ABC sitcom? `2 points`
    a) *South Central*
    b) *Roe*
    c) *In the House*
    d) *Thea*

". . . WHEN I GET MAD, I PUT IT DOWN ON A PAD" (SONGWRITING)

This section is dedicated to the great songwriters who have given the backbone (and backbeat) to black music over the years. Don't worry, we won't be asking you to pick out chords or harmonic structures . . . just act like you know that before there were samples there had to be songs to *be* sampled.

81. On which song did Tevin Campbell rap about being a "cool kid"?
    a) "Shhh"
    b) "The Most Beautiful Girl in the World"
    c) "Can We Talk"
    d) "Round and Round"

82. Which young R&B diva cowrote hits for Mary J. Blige, including "You Gotta Believe"?

a) Faith Evans
b) Brandy
c) Aaliyah
d) Diane Warren

83. In 1995, producer Babyface wrote which Number One Madonna record?

a) "Ray of Light"
b) "Take a Bow"
c) "Papa Don't Preach"
d) "Like a Virgin"

84. Who wrote the smash R&B hit "Juicy Fruit" before going on to write the theme music for *NY Undercover*?

a) James Mtume
b) Jimmy Jam
c) Stevie Wonder
d) Curtis Mayfield

85. Which of the following songs did Diane Warren NOT write?
    `2 points`

a) "Rhythm of the Night," by DeBarge
b) "Because You Love Me," by Celine Dion
c) "End of the Road," by Boyz II Men
d) "Unbreak My Heart," by Toni Braxton

86. Who wrote "I Have Learned to Respect the Power of Love" while still a student at Howard University? `5 points`

a) Roberta Flack
b) Toni Braxton
c) Angela Winbush
d) Crystal Waters

[Answers on page 230]

SMOKEY'S #8 PICK FOR
BEST ALBUMS OF THE 1990s:

Chronic 2001, *Dr. Dre (2000)*

"Things just ain't the same for gangstas/Times is changin', young niggas is agin'." Growing up in hip-hop is a difficult thing to do, especially when you're Dr. Dre and your sonic vocabulary has defined a whole era of hip-hop history. But this follow-up to the fabled Chronic *album did what many thought could never happen: It brought back G-funk with a contemporary feel, once again made Dre's L.A. the center of the rap game, and found someone with more charisma than Snoop Doggy Dogg: Eminem.*

Essential tracks: "Xxplosive" and "Forgot About Dre."

MARY J. BLIGE

I'M STILL #1 (ARTISTS ON THE CHARTS)

87. In 1991, which band's *EFIL4ZAGGIN* topped the *Billboard* charts?

a) Jamiroquai
b) N.W.A
c) Westside Connection
d) A Tribe Called Quest

88. Which former cheerleader's triple-platinum debut album sold more records than her next three albums combined? `2 points`

a) Michel'le
b) Paula Abdul
c) Lisa Stansfield
d) Jody Watley

89. In 1996, No Limit CEO Master P received huge national radio and video airplay for which song? `2 points`

a) "Danger"
b) "Ice-Cream Man"
c) "Make 'Em Say Uggh!"
d) "Ghetto D"

JUST ME AND YOU (DUETS)

90. Mary J. Blige and Jay-Z teamed up for which 1996 opening album cut?

a) "All I Need"
b) "Can't Knock the Hustle"
c) "Hard Knock Life (Ghetto Anthem)"
d) "Sunshine"

SCOTT'S #**7** PICK FOR BEST SINGLES OF THE 1990s:

"Rock Dis Funky Joint," Poor Righteous Teachers (1990)

The best of the early-nineties prophet raps. Swing your Africa medallion and be proud.

[Answers on page 230]

SNOOP DOGGY DOGG

91. On which album did Aaliyah duet with both Slick Rick and Treach?

a) *One in a Million*
b) *Age Ain't Nothin' but a Number*
c) *Romeo Must Die* soundtrack
d) *Supa Dupa Fly*

92. In 1999, who duetted with the Roots on their hit single, "You Got Me"?

a) Amel Larrieux
b) Erykah Badu
c) Lauryn Hill
d) Vinia Mojica

BONUS INTERNET QUESTION: Who originally wrote and performed the song's hook?

93. Method Man has NOT duetted with which artist?

a) Mary J. Blige
b) Redman
c) Eminem
d) Foxy Brown

94. Snoop first teamed up with Dr. Dre on which soundtrack?

a) *Gridlock'd*
b) *Poetic Justice*
c) *Deep Cover*
d) *Beverly Hills Cop III*

SMOKEY'S #**7** PICK FOR
BEST SINGLES OF THE 1990s:

"Dear Mama," Tupac (1995)

Dedicated to the remarkable woman who almost gave birth to her son while incarcerated as a Black Panther, "Dear Mama" became a hip-hop anthem of a different kind and has enabled 'Pac fans to forever excuse away the misogynistic, "thug life" identity their hero would later wear like a Superman outfit. Any of his disappointing lyrical choices are countered with, "But did you hear 'Dear Mama?'" "There's no way I can pay you back/But the plan is to show you that I understand." They do have a point.

(175)

What's Your HI-FI Q?

95. With which reggae star does Lauryn Hill "duet" on "Turn Your Lights Down Low"?
   a) Peter Tosh
   b) Bob Marley
   c) Shabba Ranks
   d) Patra

96. With whom did Mariah Carey duet on her 1997 rendition of Prince's "The Beautiful Ones"?
   a) Prince
   b) Dru Hill
   c) Boyz II Men
   d) 'N Sync

97. Which of the following artists has NOT duetted with Mary J. Blige?
   a) George Michael
   b) Elton John
   c) DMX
   d) Jay-Z

98. Which rapper has Mary J. Blige NOT recorded with?
   a) Grand Puba
   b) Notorious B.I.G.
   c) Queen Latifah
   d) Lil' Kim

99. Which of the following artists has NOT duetted with Janet Jackson?
   2 points
   a) Shaggy
   b) Treach
   c) Blackstreet
   d) Busta Rhymes

100. On which Michael Jackson album did the singer duet with his sister Janet? `2 points`

a) *Off the Wall*
b) *Thriller*
c) *Dangerous*
d) *HIStory*

101. Johnny Gill and Coko remade which classic duet for the *Booty Call* soundtrack? `2 points`

a) "Fire and Desire"
b) "If This World Were Mine"
c) "Endless Love"
d) "Where Is the Love"

REMAKES & COVERS

102. Who remade a Smokey Robinson song with these lyrics: "And if you want it, you got it forever/This is not a one-night stand"?

a) Maxwell
b) D'Angelo
c) Ginuwine
d) Usher

103. With whom did Luther Vandross remake "Endless Love"?

a) Diana Ross
b) Mariah Carey
c) Whitney Houston
d) Anita Baker

FUGEES

104. Who sang vocals on Nas's 1996 interpolation of Kurtis Blow's "If I Ruled the World"?

- a) Aaliyah
- b) Mary J. Blige
- c) Lauryn Hill
- d) Faith Evans

105. Which 15-year-old songstress remade Marvin Gaye's "Got to Give It Up" on her 1994 debut album?

- a) Christina Aguilera
- b) Aaliyah
- c) Brandy
- d) Erykah Badu

106. On 1996's *The Score*, the Fugees covered which two artists' most adored singles?

- a) Prince and Roberta Flack
- b) Marvin Gaye and Bob Marley
- c) Bob Marley and Roberta Flack
- d) Bob Dylan and Teddy Pendergrass

107. In 1996, Nice & Smooth teamed up with C+C Music Factory for a remake of which Cheryl Lynn hit?

- a) "I Will Survive"
- b) "Encore"
- c) "If This World Were Mine"
- d) "Got to Be Real"

108. In 1992, Whitney Houston wowed screen audiences with her rendition of "I Will Always Love You," a song written and originally performed by whom?

- a) Babyface
- b) Sheena Easton
- c) Dolly Parton
- d) Diana Ross

[Answers on page 230]

What's Your HI-FI Q?

109. Which Prince-composed song was NOT recorded by TLC? `2 points`

a) "If I Was Your Girlfriend"
b) "The Beautiful Ones"
c) "Get It Up"
d) "Waterfalls"

110. In 1990, Soul II Soul producer Nellee Hooper produced which Prince remake? `2 points`

a) "When Doves Cry"
b) "Nothing Compares 2 U"
c) "1999"
d) "Creep"

111. Which of the following classics did NOT appear on *Songs*, Luther Vandross's album of cover songs? `2 points`

a) "Love the One You're With"
b) "Endless Love"
c) "Always and Forever"
d) "Sir Duke"

112. Which of the following artists did NOT remake Roberta Flack's "Killing Me Softly"? `2 points`

a) Luther Vandross
b) Al B. Sure!
c) the Fugees
d) Groove Theory

SCOTT'S #**6** PICK FOR BEST
SINGLES OF THE 1990s:

"Scenario," A Tribe Called Quest featuring Leaders of the New School (1991)

Simply? The best posse cut ever. Period.

113. In 1991, which artist did Mary J. Blige cover on her demo tape? `5 points`

   a) Chaka Khan
   b) Whitney Houston
   c) Anita Baker
   d) Gladys Knight

BONUS INTERNET QUESTION: Which song did Mary sing?

I WANNA BE DOWN (ARTISTS AND THEIR GROUPS)

114. In 1996, Seidah Garret took whose place as the lead vocalist of the Brand New Heavies?

   a) Caron Wheeler
   b) N'Dea Davenport
   c) Dionne Farris
   d) Gwen Stefani

115. Cold 187um and Total K-Oss are members of which rap group?

   a) Westside Connection
   b) the Dogg Pound
   c) N.W.A
   d) Above the Law

116. Sonny Cheeba and Geechi Suede are members of what Bronx, NY, duo?

   a) Run-DMC
   b) Camp Lo
   c) Kris Kross
   d) OutKast

[Answers on page 230]

SMOKEY'S **#6** PICK FOR
BEST SINGLES OF THE 1990s:

"Mind Playing Tricks on Me,"
the Geto Boys (1991)

"At night I can't sleep, I toss and turn/Candlesticks in the dark, visions of bodies being burned." Sometimes the poetry of the streets can be a little too real. For Scarface and Willie D, the reality of partner Bushwick Bill being shot in the face by his girlfriend must have motivated some of this ghetto-induced paranoia. Or maybe not. But the most frightening reality of gangsta rap's best song is that the lyrics still resonate.

BUSTA RHYMES

117. Ed O.G. of "I Got to Have It" fame rolled with which crew?

a) Da Brat Pack
b) Ruff Ryders
c) Big Dog Pit Bulls
d) Da Bulldogs

118. Which of the following artists did NOT come from Long Island, N.Y.?

a) Mariah Carey
b) Busta Rhymes
c) Jill Scott
d) Das EFX

119. Busta Rhymes was originally a member of which rap group?

a) the Jungle Brothers
b) Leaders of the New School
c) Poor Righteous Teachers
d) OutKast

120. Dionne Farris was originally a member of what group?

a) Sista
b) Jade
c) Arrested Development
d) Digable Planets

121. Musician Raphael Saadiq was formerly a member of which Oakland-based singing group?

a) Shai
b) Boyz II Men
c) Tony! Toni! Toné!
d) Mint Condition

SCOTT'S #**6** PICK FOR BEST ALBUMS OF THE 1990s:

One for All, *Brand Nubian (1990)*

The debut of the decade, Grand Puba and crew set the tone for a new kind of rap music: religious yet randy, political yet poignant, sensible yet sexy, dignified yet danceable. Africa medallions and dreadlocks, Five Percent and fever dreams, no other album so personifies the early nineties transfiguration of hip-hop as culture. And it's damn fun to boot.

Essential tracks: "All Four One" and "Slow Down."

[Answers on page 230]

R. KELLY

122. Afrika "Baby" Bambaataa is a member of which group?

a) the Zulu Nation
b) X-Clan
c) the Jungle Brothers
d) the Cold Crush Brothers

123. Which group is NOT a member of the Native Tongues?

a) De La Soul
b) the Roots
c) the Jungle Brothers
d) A Tribe Called Quest

124. R. Kelly was originally partnered with which R&B group?

a) Public Announcement
b) Jodeci
c) Boyz II Men
d) H-Town

125. Five years before his "Come Baby Come" smash, K7 was a member of which Latin freestyle group?

a) the Latin Kings
b) C+C Music Factory
c) TKA
d) Rocksteady Crew

126. Before producers Thomas McElroy and Denzil Foster spearheaded En Vogue, they were members of which group?

a) the Time
b) Force MDs
c) Club Nouveau
d) All-4-One

SMOKEY'S #6 PICK FOR BEST ALBUMS OF THE 1990s:

R. Kelly, *R. Kelly* (1995)

Trying to find his own answer to the ubiquitous sex-vs.-love, sacred-vs.-profane question that haunted so many of his musical forefathers, R. Kelly places "The Sermon" next to "Hump Bounce" and produces a classic. While his "you remind me of my Jeep" lyrics turned many casual listeners off, a closer inspection reveals the kind of songwriting that would make Stevie proud and is the first example of the work of a contemporary master.

Essential tracks: "I Can't Sleep Baby (If I)" and "Down Low (Nobody Has to Know)."

[Answers on page 230]

What's Your HI-FI Q?

127. Ginuwine, Missy Elliott, and Timbaland were originally part of which Virginia hip-hop collective? `2 points`
a) the Roots
b) Da Bassment
c) Death Row
d) Guy

128. Claude McKnight, older brother of R&B balladeer Brian McKnight, was a member of which gospel-inspired vocal group? `2 points`
a) Sounds of Blackness
b) Take 6
c) Kirk Franklin and the Family
d) the Winans

129. For which group did Martha Wash NOT record? `2 points`
a) C+C Music Factory
b) Black Box
c) Snap
d) Two Tons O' Fun

130. Who was in the short-lived group the Commission with the Notorious B.I.G.? `5 points`
a) Jay-Z and Charli Baltimore
b) Lil' Cease and Lil' Kim
c) Lil' Kim and Jay-Z
d) Lil' Kim and Puff Daddy

SCOTT'S #**5** PICK FOR BEST
SINGLES OF THE 1990s:

"Put Your Hands Where My Eyes Can See," Busta Rhymes (1998)

A truly new-sounding rap record when it came out. Still commands attention.

MY MANS AND THEM . . . (GUEST APPEARANCES)

131. Which two artists were first heard on Main Source's seminal "Live at the Barbeque"?

a) C.L. Smooth and Prodigy
b) Mase and Cam'ron
c) DMX and Jadakiss
d) Nasty Nas and Akinyele

132. In 1993, Salt-n-Pepa teamed up with which vocal quartet for their hit "Whatta Man"?

a) TLC
b) Take 6
c) Boyz II Men
d) En Vogue

133. Case's hit "Touch Me Tease Me" featured which hip-hop guest star?

a) Lil' Kim
b) Queen Pen
c) Foxy Brown
d) Pepa

134. In 1990, South Central rap heroine Yo Yo first appeared on the track "It's a Man's World" from which LP?

a) *You Can't Play Wit' My Yo Yo*
b) *AmeriKKKa's Most Wanted*
c) *Doggystyle*
d) *The Chronic*

135. Branford Marsalis performed a sax solo on which pop/R&B hit? **5 points**

a) "Sittin' Up in My Room"
b) "I Like Your Smile"
c) "On Bended Knee"
d) "Creep"

[Answers on page 230]

SMOKEY'S #**5** PICK FOR
BEST SINGLES OF THE 1990s:

"D'Evils," Jay-Z (1996)

Combine DJ Premier's piano-driven melody and knack for lyric-chopping with Jay-Z's cinematic tale-telling and the results will be memorable. While this kind of laid-back, gangsta identity will make Jay a superstar in a few short years, it will take him a long time to match the frankness of this early rhyme; "Throughout my junior high years it was all friendly/But now this higher learning got the Remy in me/Liquors invaded my kidneys/Got me ready to lick off/Mama, forgive me."

DR. DRE

136. Dr. Dre was a guest MC on which Teddy Riley—produced smash hit?

    a) "Remember the Time"
    b) "Make the Music"
    c) "Teddy's Jam"
    d) "No Diggity"

137. In 1992, which producer added a guest verse to his remix of House of Pain's biggest hit, "Jump Around"?

    a) Puff Daddy
    b) Pete Rock
    c) Timbaland
    d) Marley Marl

138. Which of these artists NEVER recorded for Uptown Records?

    a) Mary J. Blige
    b) Puff Daddy
    c) Guy
    d) Jodeci

139. Which raw hip-hop star posed seminude with Madonna in her 1992 *Sex* book?

    a) L.L. Cool J
    b) Special Ed
    c) Big Daddy Kane
    d) Biz Markie

140. Which producer was featured on the first hit single by Destiny's Child?

    a) Puff Daddy
    b) Wyclef Jean
    c) Teddy Riley
    d) Jermaine Dupri

FOXY BROWN

141. Which rapper appeared on the following two nineties rock albums: R.E.M.'s *Out of Time* and Too Much Joy's *Cereal Killers?* `2 points`

   a) L.L. Cool J
   b) KRS-One
   c) Q-Tip
   d) Ice Cube

142. Rap diva Foxy Brown appeared on which R&B remix?

   a) "Real Love"
   b) "You're Makin' Me High"
   c) "4, 3, 2, 1"
   d) "Ladies First"

143. Who did NOT appear on the remix of Brandy's "I Wanna Be Down"? `2 points`

   a) Yo Yo
   b) Queen Latifah
   c) Missy Elliott
   d) MC Lyte

144. Which 1991 rap remix features an artist who passed away before the song was released? `5 points`

   a) "Dear Mama"
   b) "Scenario"
   c) "They Reminisce Over You (T.R.O.Y.)"
   d) "Still Not a Player"

BONUS INTERNET QUESTION: Can you name the artist?

SALT-N-PEPA

WHERE I'M COMING FROM (ARTISTS' HOMETOWNS)

145. Mary J. Blige grew up in the "Slow Bomb" projects of which waterfront city?

a) Brooklyn, NY
b) Compton, CA
c) Long Beach, CA
d) Yonkers, NY

146. Staten Island, N.Y.C.'s "fifth" borough, is home to which two groups?

a) Wu-Tang Clan and Force MDs
b) Wu-Tang Clan and Boyz II Men
c) Boyz II Men and Village People
d) the Supremes and Destiny's Child

147. Politically engaged rap group the Coup hails from which city?

a) Oakland
b) St. Louis
c) Compton
d) San Diego

148. The group Dru Hill took its name from which Baltimore, MD, neighborhood? `2 points`

a) Druid Hill Projects
b) Dru Hill Road
c) Drew Barrymore Avenue
d) the West Side

JAY-Z

149. Los Angeles' Freestyle Fellowship honed their artistic and lyrical skills at which underground café? `5 points`

a) the Blue Note
b) the Nuyorican Poets Cafe
c) the Good Life
d) Mosque #7

YOU CAN GET WITH THIS OR YOU CAN GET WITH THAT (ANALOGIES)

150. Head-wrap queen Erykah Badu is to Wright as Brooklyn-born Jay-Z is to:

a) Combs
b) Simmons
c) Dash
d) Carter

151. Berry Gordy is to Motown as Puff Daddy is to:

a) Uptown
b) Bad Boy
c) Def Jam
d) Tommy Boy

152. Berry Gordy is to Mahogany as Ice Cube is to:

a) *Friday*
b) *The Players Club*
c) *Anaconda*
d) *Boyz N the Hood*

ICE CUBE

153. **Aaliyah is to *Romeo Must Die* as Brandy is to:**
   a) *I Still Know What You Did Last Summer*
   b) *Rodgers and Hammerstein's Cinderella*
   c) *Double Platinum*
   d) *Osmosis Jones*

154. **Jay-Z's "Hard Knock Life" is to *Annie* as Flipmode Squad's "What You Come Around Here For" is to:**
   a) *Dream Girls*
   b) *Cats*
   c) *Oliver*
   d) *Rent*

155. **Bunny is to El as Brandy is to:**
   a) Stevie J
   b) Ray J
   c) Jay-Z
   d) Eazy-E

156. **"(Shoop Shoop)" is to "Exhale" as "(Love)" is to:**
   a) "Superwoman"
   b) "Spanish Guitar"
   c) "Don't Let Go"
   d) "He Wasn't Man Enough for Me"

157. **Angela Bassett is to Tina Turner as Theresa Randle is to:**
   a) Diana Ross
   b) Natalie Cole
   c) Kathy Sledge
   d) La Toya Jackson

BOYZ II MEN

158. Kelly Price is to "Mo Money Mo Problems" as Mya is to:

a) "A Roller Skating Jam Named Saturdays"
b) "Ghetto Supastar (That Is What You Are)"
c) "All About the Benjamins"
d) "Ride Wit' Me"

159. Wanya Morris is to "Brokenhearted" as Johnny Gill is to:

a) "Perfect Combination"
b) "N.E. Heartbreak"
c) "Candy Girl"
d) "Brown Sugar"

160. Maxwell is to "Fortunate" as Michael Jackson is to: `2 points`

a) "She's Out of My Life"
b) "In the Closet"
c) "Scandalous"
d) "You Are Not Alone"

161. "Buddy" is to De La Soul as "It's All Good" is to: `2 points`

a) DMX
b) Public Enemy
c) Special Ed
d) Chubb Rock

162. Prince is to Jamie Star as Method Man is to: `2 points`

a) Wu-Tang Clan
b) Staten Island, NY
c) Ghostface Killah
d) Johnny Blaze

LAURYN HILL

163. R. Kelly's "Gotham City" is to *Batman & Robin* as "I Believe I Can Fly" is to: 2 points

a) *New Jack City*
b) *Forrest Gump*
c) *Independence Day*
d) *Space Jam*

164. JoJo is to K-Ci Hailey as Devante Swing is to: 2 points

a) Ginuwine
b) Mr. Dalvin
c) New Jack Swing
d) Timbaland

165. Dawn Robinson is to En Vogue as Bobby Brown is to: 2 points

a) Levert
b) Shai
c) New Edition
d) Boyz II Men

166. Lalah is to Donny as Nona is to: 2 points

a) Marvin
b) Jermaine
c) Teddy
d) Hendryx

167. Lauryn Hill is to the Fugees as Jody Watley is to: 2 points

a) Destiny's Child
b) Shalamar
c) S.O.S. Band
d) Labelle

What's Your HI-FI Q?

168. Grandmaster Flash is to *The Chris Rock Show* as Kid Capri is to: `5 points`
    a) *Def Comedy Jam*
    b) *In Living Color*
    c) *Roc*
    d) *Saturday Night Live*

169. "Why You Wanna Treat Me So Bad" is to the Luniz as "I Got 5 on It" is to: `5 points`
    a) 112
    b) Boyz II Men
    c) Puff Daddy
    d) Joe

RESPECT YOUR ROOTS (SAMPLES)

170. Spandau Ballet's "True" laid the musical background for which 1991 hit?
    a) "It Was a Good Day"
    b) "Bonita Applebum"
    c) "That's the Way Love Goes"
    d) "Set Adrift on Memory Bliss"

171. Edie Brickell's "What I Am" laid the musical groundwork for which hip-hop group's most successful single? `2 points`
    a) Public Enemy
    b) Fugees
    c) Brand Nubian
    d) the LOX

172. Which of these songs samples Jimi Hendrix? `2 points`

a) Puff Daddy's "All About the Benjamins"
b) The Pharcyde's "Passin' Me By"
c) A Tribe Called Quest's "Hot Sex"
d) Arrested Development's "People Everyday"

173. Naughty by Nature's 1991 anthem "O.P.P." sampled which song? `2 points`

a) "Wanna Be Startin' Somethin'"
b) "Bad"
c) "I Want You Back"
d) "ABC"

BONUS INTERNET QUESTION: Name three other nineties records that sampled the same song.

174. In 1993, Black Moon remixed their song "I Gotcha Opin" using which soul-man sample? `2 points`

a) "Playing Your Game Baby," by Barry White
b) "What's Going On," by Marvin Gaye
c) "Love TKO," by Teddy Pendergrass
d) "Tears of a Clown," by Smokey Robinson

175. Jay-Z sampled which Queens MC for the hook to his debut single, "Dead Presidents"? `2 points`

a) Rakim
b) Nas
c) L.L. Cool J
d) Run-DMC

SMOKEY'S #**5** PICK FOR BEST ALBUMS OF THE 1990s:

Illmatic, *Nas (1994)*

17-year-old Nasir Jones, still living in the Queensbridge Housing Projects his music grew out of, painted one of the most moving portraits of inner-city life ever put to record. His nihilistic lyrics were matched only by the bleakness of his young spirit.

Essential tracks: "Life's a Bitch" and "One Love."

What's Your HI-FI Q?

176. Which song is built around a sample of the Gap Band's "Outstanding?" `2 points`

a) Xscape's "Just Kickin' It"
b) Soul for Real's "Every Little Thing I Do"
c) Bobby Brown's "Every Little Step"
d) Az Yet's "Last Night"

177. From which movie did 2 Live Crew get the 1992 "Me So Horny" sample? `2 points`

a) *Full Metal Jacket*
b) *Purple Rain*
c) *Saturday Night Fever*
d) *Taboo V*

178. A Tribe Called Quest's 1990 "Youthful Expression" cut was based on which sample? `2 points`

a) "Let's Get It On"
b) "Buddy"
c) "Inner City Blues (Make Me Wanna Holler)"
d) "You're the First, the Last, My Everything"

179. De La Soul's "Keeping the Faith" sampled which Rastaman classic? `5 points`

a) "Could You Be Loved"
b) "No Woman, No Cry"
c) "Mr. Loverman"
d) "Ting-a-ling"

180. Which record did NOT sample Mary Jane Girls' "All Night Long"? `5 points`

a) "More and More Hits," Nice & Smooth
b) "Love No Limit," Mary J. Blige
c) "Tell Me," Groove Theory
d) "Juicy," Notorious B.I.G.

SCOTT'S **#4** PICK FOR BEST SINGLES OF THE 1990s:

"Remember the Time," Michael Jackson (1991)

Teddy Riley's finest post-Guy moment, in my humble opinion. Teddy gave MJ a groove so sleek, MJ could only do what he does best: lace it with an amazing vocal performance. A simple love song made complex by the MJ mystique.

181. Which rap song sampled the guitar solo from Prince's "Let's Go Crazy"?
    a) "A Roller Skating Jam Named Saturdays," De La Soul
    b) "Brothers Gonna Work It Out," Public Enemy
    c) "Get at Me Dog," DMX
    d) "Hail Mary," Makaveli

LIGHTS, CAMERA, ACTION (MUSIC VIDEOS AND HOLLYWOOD BLOCKBUSTERS)

182. TLC, Valerie Simpson, and Chaka Khan appear in which Whitney Houston video?
    a) "I'm Every Woman"
    b) "Run to You"
    c) "Saving All My Love for You"
    d) "I Wanna Dance With Somebody"

183. With whom did Jennifer Lopez tango in one of his videos?
    a) Busta Rhymes
    b) Usher
    c) Puff Daddy
    d) Montell Jordan

184. Which of these artists has appeared in a movie with Whoopi Goldberg?
    a) Jennifer Lopez
    b) Lauryn Hill
    c) Lil' Kim
    d) Will Smith

SMOKEY'S #4 PICK FOR BEST SINGLES OF THE 1990s:

"I Believe I Can Fly," R. Kelly (1996)

Perhaps the best true ballad composed by a member of the "hip-hop generation." R. Kelly focused all of his sex-energy passion into a song of promise and motivation. The ghetto has never sounded so full of hope, and now high school graduations, the world over, can forever be free of "The Greatest Love of All." And that's saying a lot.

[Answers on page 231]

JANET JACKSON

185. Which of these artists has NOT appeared in a John Singleton film?

a) Janet Jackson
b) Busta Rhymes
c) L.L. Cool J
d) Tyrese

186. In which 1997 music video did Puff Daddy fall off a motorcycle?

a) "It's All About the Benjamins"
b) "I'll Be Missing You"
c) "P.E. 2000"
d) "Mo Money Mo Problems"

187. In which TLC video do the girls play strip poker with male models?

a) "Red Light Special"
b) "Baby-Baby-Baby"
c) "Creep"
d) "No Scrubs"

188. In which video did Janet Jackson's newly sculpted body make its first appearance?

a) "Rhythm Nation"
b) "Again"
c) "Love Will Never Do Without You"
d) "Scream"

189. Sade's "No Ordinary Love" is the theme song to which 1992 motion picture?

a) *Unforgiven*
b) *Indecent Proposal*
c) *The Piano*
d) *Sleepless in Seattle*

What's Your HI-FI Q?

190. Which model/actor appeared in Janet's 1993 "Again" video?
    a) Gary Dourdan
    b) Tyson Beckford
    c) Boris Kodjoe
    d) Iman

191. Which "Mama" song also appeared on a movie soundtrack?
    a) "Mama Said Knock You Out," by L.L. Cool J
    b) "A Song for Mama," by Boyz II Men
    c) "Dear Mama," by Tupac Shakur
    d) "Mama Said," by Lenny Kravitz

192. On which soundtrack did Whitney Houston duet with CeCe Winans?
    a) *The Bodyguard*
    b) *The Preacher's Wife*
    c) *Waiting to Exhale*
    d) *The Prince of Egypt*

193. Cypress Hill's "How I Could Just Kill a Man" was used in which Ernest Dickerson film?
    a) *Boyz N the Hood*
    b) *New Jack City*
    c) *Panther*
    d) *Juice*

194. In 1995, which actress appeared in the video for Coolio's Grammy-winning song "Gangsta's Paradise"?
    a) Sharon Stone
    b) Michelle Pfeiffer
    c) Jennifer Lopez
    d) Kim Basinger

195. Which of the following rappers has NOT been a major movie star? 2 points

a) Tupac Shakur
b) DMX
c) Notorious B.I.G.
d) Ice Cube

196. On which soundtrack did Mary J. Blige debut? 2 points

a) *Girl 6*
b) *Menace II Society*
c) *Strictly Business*
d) *Juice*

197. Which of the following celebrities did NOT appear in Michael Jackson's "Remember the Time" video? 2 points

a) Magic Johnson
b) Naomi Campbell
c) Eddie Murphy
d) Iman

198. Which historically black fraternity was featured in the video to Chubb Rock's hit single "Just the Two of Us"? 2 points

a) Omega Psi Phi
b) Delta Sigma Theta
c) Kappa Alpha Psi
d) Phi Beta Sigma

199. In which 1991 music video does Michael Jackson get to play under Michael Jordan's legs? 2 points

a) "Jam"
b) "In the Closet"
c) "Wanna Be Startin' Somethin'"
d) "Remember the Time"

[Answers on pages 231–232]

SMOKEY'S #4 PICK FOR
BEST ALBUMS OF THE 1990s:

It's Dark and Hell Is Hot, *DMX* (1998)

A lifetime of suffering in the making. Earl Simmons's debut Bible ended hip-hop's shiny-suit game and reminded us all of the real struggles within America's inner cities. His are the stories the music claims to represent. Where Earl felt pain, X brought anger—a man's disappointment leading to a rapper's aggression. Who's afraid of the dark?

Essential tracks: "Get At Me Dog," "Ruff Ryders Anthem," and "Let Me Fly."

TUPAC SHAKUR

200. Who sang jazz standards in the film *Living Out Loud*? `2 points`

a) Queen Latifah
b) R. Kelly
c) Gerald Levert
d) Toni Braxton

201. Which was the last video Tupac Shakur made before his death? `2 points`

a) "California Love"
b) "I'll Be Around"
c) "To Live and Die in L.A."
d) "Hail Mary"

202. In Junior M.A.F.I.A.'s "Get Money" video, which almost-recording artist donned a blond wig? `5 points`

a) Lil' Kim
b) Foxy Brown
c) Yo Yo
d) Charli Baltimore

COVER TO COVER (ARTISTS IN NEWSPAPERS AND MAGAZINES)

203. Which of the following artists has NEVER been on the cover of *VIBE* magazine?

a) Sisqó
b) Ice Cube
c) Lil' Kim
d) Bobby Brown

204. Which artist told *VIBE*, "It doesn't bother me that people think we aren't great singers. At least they're thinking of us enough to talk about [us]"?

a) Pam of Total
b) Coko of SWV
c) Chili of TLC
d) Beyoncé of Destiny's Child

[Answers on page 232]

What's Your HI-FI Q?

205. Who said this to *Rolling Stone* about working with Dr. Dre: "I'm a brat, and so is he . . . he got the formula and I got mine. And we was clashin'"?

a) Snoop Dogg
b) Eve
c) Eminem
d) Michel'le

206. Which artist told *VIBE*, "Black people haven't had anything like us in a while. This group's saying something about police brutality, the government, social issues, *and* straight-up hip-hop"?

a) Posdnuos of De La Soul
b) Wyclef of the Fugees
c) Grand Puba of Brand Nubian
d) Willie D of the Geto Boys

207. Who told *Ebony* magazine, "Guys pretty much can be in some jeans and say whatever they want to say. We're the real trendsetters. You have a lot of young female teenagers who look up to us and want to be sassy like we are"?

a) Eve
b) Missy Elliott
c) Lil' Kim
d) Foxy Brown

208. Who told *Ebony* magazine, "With this album I want to tell the brothers that if you have someone at home, just take care of her. Thugs fall in love too"?

a) Dave Hollister
b) Ja Rule
c) Jahiem
d) D'Angelo

SCOTT'S #**3** PICK FOR BEST
SINGLES OF THE 1990s:

*"Mo Money Mo Problems,"
Notorious B.I.G. featuring Puff
Daddy (1997)*

The best of the Puffy bunch to dominate radio and clubs in the late nineties. Perfect use of a sample loop. Crazily addictive to the ear and ass.

209. In 1996 *People* magazine profiled which performer under the headline "Going Broke on $30 Million a Year"?
   a) Bill Cosby
   b) M.C. Hammer
   c) Michael Jackson
   d) Milli Vanilli

210. Who is the only non-recording artist to have ever appeared solo on the cover of *The Source* magazine?
   a) Suge Knight
   b) Russell Simmons
   c) Berry Gordy, Jr.
   d) Master P

211. Which rap artist appeared on the covers of *VIBE, Rolling Stone,* and *Newsweek* BEFORE the release of his debut album?
   a) Puff Daddy
   b) Notorious B.I.G.
   c) 2Pac
   d) Snoop Doggy Dogg

212. Which group told *Spin,* "In our neighborhood, you either played sports or entertained in some way—even if that meant entertaining by seeing how much stuff you could steal"?
   a) Run of Run-DMC
   b) Phife of A Tribe Called Quest
   c) King Lou of Dream Warriors
   d) Mr. Lawnge of Black Sheep

213. Who told *VIBE,* "In '87–'88, I was rich. In '89, I was broke . . . can't-buy-gas, sell-the-car broke"? `2 points`
   a) L.L. Cool J
   b) Slick Rick
   c) Will Smith
   d) Big Daddy Kane

[Answers on page 232]

SMOKEY'S #**3** PICK FOR
BEST SINGLES OF THE 1990s:

"Put Your Hands Where My Eyes Could See," Busta Rhymes (1997)

Somehow bridging the gap between the tribal beats of the music's African roots and the booty-shakin' contemporary moment, Busa Bus gave us arguably the funkiest three minutes hip-hop has ever heard. Or maybe it was just a great sample. Either way, this self-proclaimed "dungeon dragon" held back the roaring for a minute to play games with the rhyme. "Hit you wit' no delayin', so what you sayin' yo?/Silly with my nine milli, what the dealie, yo?" Classic.

What's Your
HI-FI Q?

SCOTT'S #**3** PICK FOR BEST
ALBUMS OF THE 1990s:

CrazySexyCool, *TLC (1994)*

On which the little girls grow up, behave themselves, and make a classic for their times, this was the third best of the Follow-Up Class of 1994. This record did something records rarely do nowadays in these hit-hungry times of ours: It had six producers, and yet one vision—the artists'—prevailed. Babyface and Dallas Austin gave the women their best, and the women didn't let them down. This is also one of the few albums of the nineties that demanded to be represented with videos. There's a cinematic ease to how these women materialize into the ether and never leave the inner ear satisfied.

Essential tracks: "Creep" and "Waterfalls."

214. Who told *VIBE*, "For all the girls who are too shy to tell their men how they feel, I'm here to help them out"? `2 points`
    a) Jennifer Lopez
    b) Monica
    c) Adina Howard
    d) Miss Jones

MUST NOT BE THE MUSIC (LYRICS)

215. Which rapper first spoke of sporting "Tommy Hilfiger top gear"?
    a) Grand Puba
    b) Q-Tip
    c) Erick Sermon
    d) Jay-Z

216. Name the song with these lyrics: "See we be makin' love constantly/That's why my eyes are a shade blood burgundy."
    a) "Back at One"
    b) "You Make Me Wanna"
    c) "The Thong Song"
    d) "Brown Sugar"

217. Who knew he "was dope ever since [he] was semen/swimmin' in [his] daddy's big nuts"?
    a) Q-Tip
    b) Grand Puba
    c) Redman
    d) Ol' Dirty Bastard

218. On Mary J. Blige's first single "You Remind Me," she wondered, "is it a dream or is it . . ."

a) "my sad life"
b) "the look between me and you"
c) "déjà vu"
d) "a beautiful blue"

219. On her second album, Mary J. Blige sang, "all I really want is to"?

a) " . . . get money"
b) " . . . be happy"
c) " . . . to find someone that loves me"
d) " . . . to be free"

220. Who went "raaaw, raaaw, like a dungeon dragon" on 1991's "Scenario"?

a) Ol' Dirty Bastard
b) Big Daddy Kane
c) Busta Rhymes
d) Mystikal

221. According to Treach, in "O.P.P." there's "no room for relationships, there's just" what?

a) "room to breathe"
b) "room to hit it"
c) "room to rent it"
d) "time to chill"

222. For Ce Ce Peniston in 1992 "it happened to me" when?

a) "finally"
b) "eventually"
c) "soon enough"
d) "in reality"

SMOKEY'S #3 PICK FOR
BEST ALBUMS OF THE 1990s:

Life After Death, *Notorious B.I.G.* (1997)

This quintessential document of nineties urban culture incorporates all of the violence, suffering, and bling-bling dreams that the hip-hop generation deals with on a daily basis. Biggie underscored his ghetto consciousness with the kind of lyrical creativity that has yet to be matched.

Essential tracks: "Hypnotize" and "Ten Crack Commandments."

[Answers on page 232]

A TRIBE CALLED QUEST

223. In 1990, where did A Tribe Called Quest leave their wallet?
   a) on the #2 train
   b) with Bonita Applebum
   c) on their instinctive travels
   d) in El Segundo

224. What have the lovers "made it through" in Mary J. Blige's "Real Love"?
   a) "the storm"
   b) "the fire"
   c) "the sheets"
   d) "the worst it gets"

225. On what 1993 hit did Missy Elliott wail "Hee hee hee hee, haw"?
   a) "Steelo," by 702
   b) "Can We," by SWV
   c) "The Things You Do," by Gina Thompson
   d) "The Rain (Supa Dupa Fly)," by Missy Elliott

226. According to the Eminem hit, "Will the Real Slim Shady, please" do what?
   a) "stand up"
   b) "shut up"
   c) "move up"
   d) "get busy"

227. "It's funny how money change a situation" is the first line to which song?
   a) "My Way," by Usher
   b) "Nobody's Supposed to Be Here," by Deborah Cox
   c) "Lost Ones," by Lauryn Hill
   d) "It's All About the Benjamins," by Puff Daddy and the Family

[Answers on page 232]

What's Your HI-FI Q?

228. "Like a moth to a flame, burned by the fire" is the first line to which hit song?

    a) "Escapade," by Janet Jackson
    b) "That's the Way Love Goes," by Janet Jackson
    c) "The Boy Is Mine," by Brandy and Monica
    d) "Bootylicious," by Destiny's Child

229. The Lost Boyz rhyme about the "Lifestyles of the" what?

    a) "rich and gameless"
    b) "rich and shameless"
    c) "rich and nameless"
    d) "rich and blameless"

230. Who has a "one-track mind" on Diamond D's 1992 album *Stunts, Blunts & Hip-Hop*?

    a) Shorty
    b) Molly
    c) Sally
    d) Chuck D

231. Del tha Funkeehomosapien hit it big in 1991 with the song "Mistadobalina." What was the character's first name?

    a) Rob
    b) Tom
    c) Bob
    d) Job

232. In 1995, which Atlanta-based rap quartet worried "someone's creeping in my window"?

    a) Goodie Mob
    b) OutKast
    c) TLC
    d) Xscape

SCOTT'S #**2** PICK FOR BEST SINGLES OF THE 1990s:

"Make Sure You're Sure," Stevie Wonder (1991)

The best track from his Jungle Fever *soundtrack. Subtle, yet full of feeling. A complete thought.*

233. Who loosely covered Sly and the Family Stone's "Everyday People" with the lyrics "acting like a nigga and get stomped by an African"?

a) Arrested Development
b) Joi
c) TLC
d) Soul II Soul

234. Snoop Doggy Dogg appeared with Laurence Fishburne in the video of the title cut to which movie soundtrack?

a) Othello
b) Deep Cover
c) What's Love Got to Do With It
d) Above the Rim

235. Over three consecutive albums, which group first begged a sister to stay, cried for her, then "woke up feeling so horny"?

a) After 7
b) Levert
c) Jodeci
d) Boyz II Men

236. Who is the "chocolate boy wonder"?

a) Heavy D
b) Pete Rock
c) Puff Daddy
d) Big Daddy Kane

237. Which female group first warned women to "hold on" to their man, then two years later declared he was "never gonna get it"?

a) Gladys Knight and the Pips
b) Destiny's Child
c) SWV
d) En Vogue

[Answers on page 232]

SMOKEY'S #**2** PICK FOR BEST SINGLES OF THE 1990s:

"One More Chance," Notorious *B.I.G. (1995)*

"First things first/I, Poppa, freaks all the honies, dummies, Playboy bunnies, those wanting money." And so it began. While this wasn't Big Poppa's first single, it was certainly the one that earned him his royal moniker: King of New York. With sex-you-up lyrics as intricate as Rakim's more serious musings, B.I.G. was the artist women loved to love and brothers couldn't deny. Check his all-around game: the album version of "One More Chance" was straight hardcore rudeness, the remix featuring his then-wife Faith Evans smoothed it out on the R&B tip, while the Craig G–inspired hip-hop mix was all hardknock club. Listen to all three, and the nineties—in all of its contradiction—will be well defined.

219

NAS

238. Patti LaBelle is to Vivica A. Fox as Debbie Allen is to: `2 points`

a) Brandy
b) Maia Campbell
c) Monica
d) T-Boz

239. In 1990, which rapper declared, "when I get mad, I put it down on a pad"? `2 points`

a) Chuck D
b) Rakim
c) Nas
d) DMX

240. Which one-hit wonder scored record gold with the lines "back in the day when I was young/I'm not a kid anymore"? `2 points`

a) Ahmad
b) Special Ed
c) Young MC
d) Chi Ali

241. In Das EFX's "They Want EFX," after the "waist bone is connected to the hip bone," the hip bone is connected to what? `2 points`

a) "the thigh bone"
b) "the knee bone"
c) "the calf bone"
d) "my microphone"

242. In 1991, which Number One single sampled Slick Rick's "tick tock you don't stop" line? `2 points`

a) "No Diggity"
b) "I Wanna Sex U Up"
c) "I Want Your Sex"
d) "Rump Shaker"

SCOTT'S #2 PICK FOR BEST ALBUMS OF THE 1990s:

II, *Boyz II Men (1994)*

Another second record that built on the strengths of the first and left the weaknesses behind, Boyz II Men's follow-up to Cooleyhighharmony *emphasized the Men in its name with a potent mix of melody and attitude. In a season of R&B boy groups cropping up like weeds, Boyz II Men snagged up all the right songs, did all the right arrangements, and had all the hits. They seemed to understand that the voice should serve the song as well as the song should serve the voice. Never too much, rarely not enough, these guys knew how to strike the right chord and find the right note.*

Essential tracks: "Water Runs Dry" and "On Bended Knee."

243. Which Queens-bred rapper introduced himself to the world with the line "streets disciple/My raps are vital"? `2 points`

 a) Chuck D
 b) L.L. Cool J
 c) DMX
 d) Nas

244. In 1993, Me'Shell Ndegéocello asked her lover to "run her fingers through" what? `2 points`

 a) "your nappy head"
 b) "your baggy jeans"
 c) "your beautiful Afro"
 d) "your dred locs"

245. To what force of nature did L.L. Cool J liken himself in 1990's "Mama Said Knock U Out"? `2 points`

 a) a hurricane
 b) a twister
 c) a monsoon
 d) a storm

246. In "Hip Hop Hooray," Trench calls competing rappers' styles "older than" who? `2 points`

 a) "Barry White"
 b) "Isaac Hayes"
 c) "Lou Rawls"
 d) "my grandfather"

247. According to "Everything's Gonna Be Alright," why did Treach keep his hair in braids? **2 points**

a) "it was the style back then"
b) "I couldn't afford a haircut"
c) "'cause I was splittin' and cold-hittin' that"
d) "'cause my momma told me so"

248. "After 12," Rakim is "worse than a" what? **2 points**

a) "alien"
b) "gremlin"
c) "omen"
d) "bad habit"

249. "A lonely mother gazing out her window/Staring at a son that she just can't touch" is the first line of which hit song? **5 points**

a) "Smooth Operator," by Sade
b) "Sweet Love," by Anita Baker
c) "Waterfalls," by TLC
d) "Rhythm Nation," by Janet Jackson

250. Who did we "not understand on that Mary joint"? **5 points**

a) K-Ci Hailey
b) Craig Mack
c) Puff Daddy
d) Busta Rhymes

SMOKEY'S **#2** PICK FOR
BEST ALBUMS OF THE 1990s:

The Low End Theory, *A Tribe Called Quest (1991)*

Not as far-out as De La or as politically aggressive as P.E., Q-Tip, Phife, and producer Ali Shaheed Muhammed crafted a perfect mix of cool-jazz riffs, club-rocking snares, and witty lyrics that defined the last great moment of preplatinum hip-hop.

Essential tracks: "Check the Rhime" and "Buggin' Out."

[Answers on page 232]

MARY J. BLIGE

★

#1
Single

THE BEST SINGLE OF THE 1990s
ACCORDING TO SCOTT

"They Reminisce Over You (T.R.O.Y.)," Pete Rock and C.L. Smooth (1992)

Sad songs say so much, especially within hip-hop. C.L. Smooth structures his narratives like few other MCs, layering meaning in the mundane details of life. This is real writing— rap music that dazzles because it knows the difference between telling the truth and being honest, between keeping it real and saying what you feel. The perfect blend of rhyme and flow, nineties-style.

★

#1
Single

THE BEST SINGLE OF THE 1990s
ACCORDING TO SMOKEY

"I'll Be There for You/You're All I Need to Get By," Method Man featuring Mary J. Blige (1995)

If the nineties will be remembered as the decade hip-hop became the globe's dominant culture, then this love song by two of the community's most talented members serves as its perfect representation. It was Meth and Mary doing what Marvin and Tammi did so many years before. But this time, the pants were baggier and cornrows were wild. No one will forget the look of Meth's eyes peering over that rooftop or the power of a good rhyme and a better beat. "Shorty, I'm there for you anytime you need me . . ."

What's Your HI-FI Q?

Honorable Mention:

"Quiet Storm," Mobb Deep (1999) • "I Used To Love H.E.R.," Common (1994) • "Slippin'," DMX (1998) • "How I Could Just Kill a Man," Cypress Hill (1991) • "Ha," Juvenile (1999) • "Who Got da Props," Black Moon (1993) • "Money, Cash, Hoes," Jay-Z featuring DMX (1998)

THE BEST ALBUM OF THE 1990s ACCORDING TO SCOTT

My Life, *Mary J. Blige (1994)*

The follow-up to What's the 411, *which came before Mary started (sadly) to think of herself as a "singer/songwriter," Mary J. Blige's second album avoided the sophomore slump like the plague. Building on the ghetto-girl realness that made her debut so fresh and exciting,* My Life *felt like a diary from the front line. The pain only hinted at on her debut found its place front and center and gave Ms. Mary a gravity other post-hip-hop divas could only dream of having. This was the best of the sterling Follow-Up Class of 1994 (see below). Essential tracks: "I Love You" and "Be Happy."*

Honorable Mention:

Seal, Seal (1991) • *Seal (the second album),* (1994) • *AmeriKKKa's Most Wanted,* Ice Cube (1990) • *Cooleyhighharmony,* Boyz II Men (1991) • *Life After Death,* Notorious B.I.G. (1995) • *12 Play,* R. Kelly (1990) • *The Chronic,* Dr. Dre (1992) • *Naughty by Nature,* Naughty by Nature (1990) • *Emancipation,* Prince (1996) • *Straight Outta Hell's Kitchen,* Lisa Lisa and Cult Jam (1991)

THE BEST ALBUM OF THE 1990s ACCORDING TO SMOKEY

My Life, *Mary J. Blige (1994)*

This was only her second album, but the wonderful My Life *quickly placed Mary within the finest of R&B traditions. Her use of the music of Curtis Mayfield, Barry White, Al Green, and Roy Ayers wasn't to cover these artists, but to redefine their vocabularies for her own generation. It has never been done better. Essential tracks: "I'm the Only Woman" and "No One Else."*

Honorable Mention:

Reasonable Doubt, Jay-Z (1996) • *One for All,* Brand Nubian (1990) • *De La Soul Is Dead,* De La Soul (1991) • *Mama Said Knock You Out,* L.L. Cool J (1990) • *Mecca and the Soul Brother,* Pete Rock and C.L. Smooth (1992) • *Aquemini,* OutKast (1998) • *Love Deluxe,* Sade (1992) • *Ready 2 Die,* Notorious B.I.G. (1994) • *Emancipation,* Prince (1996)

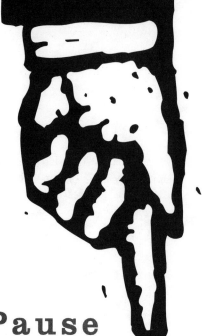

Press Pause

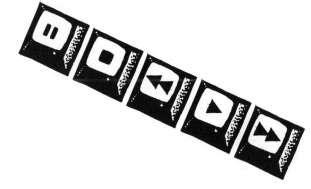

ANSWER KEY FOR THE 1990s QUESTIONS

Give yourself one point for each correct answer unless otherwise indicated. You can find answers to the Bonus Internet Questions at www.hifiq.com and www.blackbookscentral.com.

THE OPENING
1. c
2. c
3. c
4. b
5. d
6. d
7. c
8. c
9. a
10. d
11. b
12. b
13. a
14. a
15. a
16. d
17. c
18. c
19. a
20. c
21. c
22. b
23. d
24. b
25. c
26. b

27. b
28. c
29. b
30. c
31. d
32. b
33. b
34. c
35. c
36. c
37. a
38. d
39. d
40. c
41. b
42. d
43. b
44. b
45. a
46. c
47. b
48. c (2 points)
49. c (2 points)
50. c (2 points)
51. a (2 points)
52. d (2 points)
53. b (5 points)

54. c (2 points)
55. b (2 points)
56. b (2 points)
57. b (2 points)
58. c (2 points)
59. c (2 points)
60. b (2 points)
61. d (2 points)
62. c (2 points)
63. c (2 points)
64. b (2 points)
65. c (5 points)
66. c (2 points)
67. b (2 points)
68. c (2 points)
69. a (2 points)
70. b (2 points)
71. c (2 points)
72. a (2 points)
73. d (2 points)
74. b (2 points)
75. a (2 points)
76. b (5 points)
77. d (2 points)
78. a (5 points)
79. c (5 points)
80. d (2 points)

Answers

What's Your HI-FI Q?

"... WHEN I GET MAD, I PUT IT DOWN ON A PAD" (SONGWRITING)
- 81. c
- 82. a
- 83. b
- 84. a
- 85. c (2 points)
- 86. c (5 points)

I'M STILL #1 (ARTISTS ON THE CHARTS)
- 87. b
- 88. b (2 points)
- 89. b (2 points)

JUST ME AND YOU (DUETS)
- 90. b
- 91. a
- 92. b
- 93. c
- 94. c
- 95. b
- 96. b
- 97. b
- 98. c
- 99. b (2 points)
- 100. d (2 points)
- 101. a (2 points)

REMAKES & COVERS
- 102. b
- 103. a
- 104. c
- 105. b
- 106. c
- 107. d
- 108. c
- 109. b (2 points)
- 110. b (2 points)
- 111. d (2 points)
- 112. d (2 points)
- 113. c (5 points)

I WANNA BE DOWN (ARTISTS AND THEIR GROUPS)
- 114. b
- 115. d
- 116. b
- 117. d
- 118. c
- 119. b
- 120. c
- 121. c
- 122. c
- 123. b
- 124. a
- 125. c
- 126. c

- 127. b (2 points)
- 128. b (2 points)
- 129. c (2 points)
- 130. a (5 points)

MY MANS AND THEM ... (GUEST APPEARANCES)
- 131. d
- 132. d
- 133. c
- 134. b
- 135. b (5 points)
- 136. d
- 137. b
- 138. b
- 139. c
- 140. b
- 141. b (2 points)
- 142. b
- 143. c (2 points)
- 144. b (5 points)

WHERE I'M COMING FROM (ARTISTS' HOMETOWNS)
- 145. d
- 146. a
- 147. a
- 148. a (2 points)
- 149. c (5 points)

YOU CAN GET WITH THIS OR YOU CAN GET WITH THAT
(ANALOGIES)

150. d. Sean Carter is Jay-Z's proper name.
151. b. The amount Puff talks about his record label,
     this should be easy.
152. b. Cut! We wonder if either of them will release a
     director's cut DVD?
153. a. first feature-film acting roles
154. c.
155. b. brother and sister
156. c. A tough one, but the parentheses are part of
     the full song titles.
157. b. Didn't Ms. Bassett deserve an Oscar?
158. b. Someone had to sing those unforgettable
     hooks.
159. a. They sang lead on perhaps their group's
     biggest hits.
160. d. Ghetto or not, R. Kelly is a genius songwriter.
     (2 points)
161. a. Hmmm . . . We wonder why they're both songs
     about sex? (2 points)
162. d. This was pre-symbol days, but the Minneapolis
     genius was still being confusing. (2 points)
163. d. Wasn't the "Gotham City" video better than the
     movie? (2 points)
164. b. Brothers gonna work it out. (2 points)
165. c. We guess Bobby had a slightly better solo
     career. (2 points)
166. a. special father-daughter relationships (2 points)
167. b. Don't you wish this wasn't true? (2 points)
168. a. Thank Chris for this legend's better-late-than-
     never visibility. (5 points)
169. c. Sample, sample, sample . . . (5 points)

RESPECT YOUR ROOTS (SAMPLES)

170. d
171. c (2 points)
172. b (2 points)
173. c (2 points)
174. c (2 points)
175. b (2 points)
176. a (2 points)
177. a (2 points)
178. c (2 points)
179. a (5 points)
180. d (5 points)
181. b (5 points)

LIGHTS, CAMERA, ACTION (MUSIC VIDEOS AND
HOLLYWOOD BLOCKBUSTERS)

182. a
183. c
184. b
185. c
186. b
187. a
188. c
189. b
190. a
191. b
192. c
193. d
194. b
195. c (2 points)
196. c (2 points)
197. b (2 points)
198. c (2 points)

What's Your HI-FI Q?

199. a (2 points)
200. a (2 points)
201. c (2 points)
202. d (5 points)

COVER TO COVER (ARTISTS IN NEWSPAPERS AND MAGAZINES)

203. d
204. a
205. b
206. b
207. b
208. a
209. b
210. a
211. d
212. c
213. c (2 points)
214. c (2 points)

MUST NOT BE THE MUSIC (LYRICS)

215. a
216. d
217. b
218. c
219. b
220. c
221. b
222. a
223. d
224. a
225. c
226. a
227. c
228. b
229. b
230. c
231. c
232. a

233. a
234. b
235. c
236. b
237. d
238. b (2 points)
239. a (2 points)
240. a (2 points)
241. a (2 points)
242. b (2 points)
243. d (2 points)
244. d (2 points)
245. c (2 points)
246. c (2 points)
247. b (2 points)
248. b (2 points)
249. c (5 points)
250. b (5 points)

TOTAL POSSIBLE SCORE: 406 points

ENTER YOUR SCORE HERE

AND YOUR HI-FI Q IS . . .

Whew! You made it through. Don't you wanna know your HI-FI Q?

Here's how you figure it out . . .

Add up your scores from the SEVENTIES, EIGHTIES, & NINETIES.

IF YOUR TOTAL HI-FI Q SCORE IS | 0–200 |

Well . . . you have a pretty low HI-FI Q, but then again, we're guessing you already figured that out. In music industry terms you might as well consider yourself a **DEMO TAPE** that's still making the rounds to every label on the market. We'd like to think that we'd sign you at HI-FI Q Records, but, well, we like our artists a little more music savvy.

IF YOUR TOTAL HI-FI Q SCORE IS | 201–500 |

You got signed! You are a **HIT SINGLE** on HI-FI Q Records. You're getting some play on TRL; you're getting some spins on all the DJ shows; and somebody even remixed your single with a star MC guest-starring on it. A movie company wants to use it in the ad for their big summer movie. But you might wanna start moving some albums to go along with that single. With a score like yours, you might be destined for One-Hit-Wonder status.

IF YOUR TOTAL HI-FI Q SCORE IS | 501–750 |

Your hit single actually became a **GOLD** album. You've proved your metal, so to speak, and that high HI-FI Q of yours has helped you sell half a million records. Now you can go on tour and HI-FI Q Records will treat you with some respect. We'll even exercise that option to let you record a second CD.

What's Your HI-FI Q?

IF YOUR TOTAL HI-FI Q SCORE IS 751–999

You might wanna think about renegotiating that cheesy deal you signed, baby, cause at this level you're a **PLATINUM** artist. Heck, you're even **multiPLATINUM.** Go buy that Lexus jeep. Go get some custom-made jewelry. Spend a mil on that next video. Make a second CD complaining about how hard life is now that you're a big huge star.

IF YOUR TOTAL HI-FI Q SCORE IS 1000

You are a **DIAMOND** seller. You've sold 10 million units worldwide. You are officially in rarified air, the smartest, best-looking, biggest-selling artist on the globe—until the next one comes along, that is. But until then, add some more folks to your posse, build that mansion, marry that model, start that vanity label, star in that movie, and don't release another CD for five years.

But if you really think you got that much game . . .

Don't forget THE BONUS HI-FI Q INTERNET QUESTIONS!

Log on to www.hifiq.com or www.blackbookscentral.com for your chance to answer the knuckle-buster questions and win SPECIAL PRIZES.

What's Your HI-FI Q?

THE OUTRO

So, you've made your way through the book. We hope you had some fun. We hope you learned some things you didn't know. We hope you conjured up some good memories along the way. We hope you jumped up and found that old LP or CD or MP3 that made you wanna dance, sing, or get up and do your thing.

That's why we did this. Not just so you could find out your HI-FI Q, but because we know that music, as Madonna sang, brings people together.

So what's next? Well, we could tell you about the HI-FI Q board game or the HI-FI Q daily calendar or the HI-FI Q game show we hope to launch sooner than later. But we won't talk about those things just yet.

At the moment, Scott is jamming to the new Macy Gray and Smokey is blasting the new Jay-Z in his ride. And we're enjoying both because we get to just chill and listen. We don't have to interview them; we don't have to write about them. We just get to enjoy them as the brilliant musicians they are.

See, it can be rough being a music writer. There are times when you just wanna enjoy a record for what it says to you and not for what you have to say about it to meet a deadline. This project was a joy-thing for Scott and Smoke. We took our time and thought of some questions that might entertain other musicheads like us out there in the world.

Somewhere in there Smokey taught Scott about the beauty of digital music and MP3s, and Scott taught Smokey about the primal beauty of Stevie Wonder's *Innervisions*. We got to share.

Which is what we wanted to do with you.

As we prepare for *What's Your HI-FI Q 2*, we look forward to hearing from you guys. Let us know what you think at www.hifiq.com; let us know what you liked and hated; let us know what stumped you and what made you feel like a, uh, musical genius.

It's just a game. We hope you had as much fun taking the quiz as we did building it. Peace.

Press Stop